Trek to Everest

Max Landsberg and Jacquetta Megarry

Nepal consultants: Siân Pritchard-Jones and Bob Gibbons

Nuptse, seen from Kala Pattar

Rucksack Readers

Trek to Everest

Published in 2016 by Rucksack Readers,
6 Old Church Lane, Edinburgh, EH15 3PX, UK
telephone +44/0 131 661 0262
website *www.rucsacs.com*
email info@rucsacs.com

Distributed in North America by Interlink Publishing, 46 Crosby Street,
Northampton, Mass., 01060, USA (*www.interlinkbooks.com*)

ISBN 978-1-898481-72-0

British Library cataloguing in publication data: a catalogue record for this book is
available from the British Library.

Maps, illustrations and book design by Ian Clydesdale *(www.workhorse.co.uk)*.

Printed in the UK by Ashford Colour Press, on water-resistant, biodegradable paper.

Publisher's note

Individual trekkers are responsible for their own welfare and safety, and for being
properly equipped for the trail conditions. The publisher cannot accept liability
for any ill-health or injury arising directly or indirectly from reading this book. All
information has been checked carefully prior to publication. However, things may
change: always take local advice, check weather forecasts and be alert to dangers.

Please visit this book's web page *www.rucsacs.com/books/tte* for any updates;
also check our links page *www.rucsacs.com/links/tte* for multimedia resources,
porter protection, tour operators and much more.

Feedback is welcome and will be rewarded: please email info@rucsacs.com

All feedback will be followed up, and readers whose comments lead to changes are
welcome to claim a free copy of our next edition upon publication.

Contents

1 Introduction

There are many reasons to trek to Everest, some obvious, others subtler. Of the two base camps used by climbers, the only one to trek to is in Nepal, through the valleys of Sagarmāthā National Park. (Expeditions always drive to the other base camp, in Tibet.)

Many visitors will be ticking off an entry on their bucket lists: following in the footsteps of famous climbers, standing in awe of the world's highest mountain and marvelling at the snow-capped summits. The physical demands of this trek will be achievable for most, yet it's tough enough to provide a strong sense of achievement.

The Khumbu and Gokyo valleys are rich in fascinating flora and fauna. Every rhododendron in the world is descended from the indigenous Himalayan plant that you see along the trail. And at higher altitudes, the geology is increasingly exposed, with glacial lakes, moraines and snow-clad peaks.

Many trekkers are delighted by the richness of Sherpa culture. First-time visitors to Nepal expect the exotic, and on trek their expectations are exceeded. Sherpa life is attractively simple, with their commitment to hard work and their insistent *shey-shey* hospitality. The Sherpa welcome is complemented by the beauty of the Buddhist trailside heritage – *mani* stones, *stupas* and prayer wheels. All this awaits you.

Tourism is the lifeblood of Nepal's economy. To quote the late Sir Edmund Hillary: 'Tourism is a very big economic benefit to the Sherpa people, and also they have very strong ties to their own social attitudes and their own religion, so fortunately they're not too influenced by many of our Western attitudes.' The massive earthquakes that struck in 2015 killed about 9000 people and left millions more homeless. The world gave aid, the Nepalis reacted with stoicism and energy, and much of the damage has been repaired. But Nepalis need your custom now, more than ever before.

What is the best time of year?

Of Nepal's four seasons, spring or autumn are best for trekking, but expect major differences between temperatures in the Khumbu valley and Kathmandu. These mainly reflect altitude differences, which in Nepal are as important as the effect of the seasons. Your latitude will be about 28° N, similar to Miami or Cairo.

The pre-monsoon season (March to May) is popular. Days and nights are warmer, often at the price of afternoon haze – but with flowers in bloom. Kathmandu averages low temperatures of 8°C, highs of 28°C or more. Most attempts to summit Mount Everest take place in late May.

Summer is monsoon season, when strong winds sweep wet air in from the Bay of Bengal, and it usually extends from mid-June to mid-September, varying from year to year. This season is worth avoiding, because central Nepal is hot, humid and wet. In trekking areas, the weather is rainy, clouds obscure the views and the trail underfoot may be very muddy. Leeches infest altitudes up to 3500 m.

Autumn (mid-September to November) is excellent for trekking, especially late autumn when the colours may be vibrant and the skies often clear with plenty of sunshine. Although nights are cold (-5°C to -15°C at Gorak Shep), Kathmandu has daily highs of 20°C or more.

Winter is from December to February and can be foggy in the early mornings, but the trails are relatively empty. Nights are very cold (down to -20°C at Gorak Shep). The temperature in Kathmandu ranges from 2·5°C to 20°C.

At this latitude, the noonday sun is always high in the sky, and the daily temperature range is extreme year-round, with nights that are cold or very cold, especially at altitude. Rain and mist often roll in during the afternoons, and thunderstorms can occur at any time of year.

Yaks approaching a pass

The period between booking your trek and departure is important: it allows you to prepare physically for a tough hike to altitudes of well over 5000 m (16,400 ft). Consider also learning a bit about Nepal, its heritage and religions, the Sherpa people and perhaps also some phrases of Nepali before you go: see page 79. At least learn to reciprocate the *namaste* gesture with which you will be warmly greeted.

Choosing your trek

For many people, the goal and route seem obvious: fly from home to Lukla via Kathmandu, then trek to Everest Base Camp (EBC) via Namche Bazaar, and retrace your steps. We suggest that there are other interesting options to consider before you settle on an itinerary:

For some people, the cost of air travel to Nepal means that the trek may form part of a longer holiday: for some of Nepal's other attractions, see page 30.

Since (no matter what the weather) you can't see Everest's summit from its Base Camp, many people will want to climb something with a summit view: Kala Pattar is the most obvious choice, and as a side-trip from Gorak Shep it combines readily with a visit to EBC (either before or after EBC).

If you prefer a more remote experience, the trek to Gokyo Lakes has a much more beautiful destination than Base Camp, and the summit of Gokyo Ri arguably offers a better (albeit more distant) view of Everest than does Kala Pattar.

If you enjoy a greater challenge and have the extra resources, consider a circuit from Namche that takes you over the Cho La and can be combined with Kala Pattar/EBC or Gokyo Ri or both.

These options are summarised in the table below, and described in detail in Parts 3 and 4.

	duration (ascent)	highest altitude reached	comments	map pages
Lukla to EBC	**9-11 days**	**EBC 5360** **Kala Pattar 5545**	**popular choice**	**41, 43, 47, 49, 53, 56**
Lukla to Gokyo	**7-9 days**	**Gokyo 4790** **Gokyo Ri 5360**	**less busy than EBC**	**41, 43, 73, 67**
Lukla to EBC and Gokyo via the Cho La	**12-14 days**	**Cho La 5370** **Kala Pattar 5545**	**can do this clockwise or anti-clockwise**	**41, 43, 47, 49, 73, 67**

The diagram below shows you the profile of the standard route from Lukla to EBC in seven sections. Although each section can be done in a day, nobody (unless pre-acclimatised e.g. from a previous expedition) should attempt this trek in seven days: you need several extra overnights for acclimatisation, and a bare minimum of two days for descent, taking the overall duration close to a fortnight. Most operators will build in 2-3 nights at Namche Bazaar and 2-3 nights at Pheriche or Dingboche. On the 'rest' days, it's wise to spend at least a few hours trekking higher, to aid acclimatisation – or, if you feel exhausted, maybe just rest.

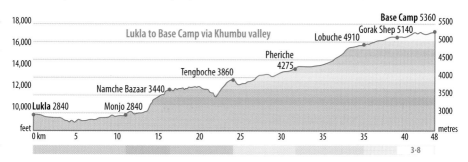

At 2840 m (9320 ft), Lukla is high enough for a few unlucky people to develop symptoms merely from flying there. (Before the airport opened, the traditional route was to take a bus from Kathmandu to Jiri, then hike for 6-9 days to join the trail near Lukla.) The profile above doesn't show the rest days: although they are essential, different groups spend different numbers of extra nights in various places.

You may need extra nights for other reasons, for example at Gorak Shep if your plans include Kala Pattar. Also, since flying into and out of Lukla is sometimes thwarted by poor weather, you may spend one or two unplanned extra nights in Kathmandu or Lukla. The timing of your international flight needs to take account of this uncertainty.

If instead you trek from Lukla to Gokyo, the altitude gain is less (Gokyo is at 4790 m whilst Gorak Shep is at 5140 m) and the distance shorter, but you still need extra overnights. If you opt to make the circuit to EBC clockwise, over the Cho La from Gokyo to Lobuche, then you can continue up the Khumbu valley to Gorak Shep and EBC. (Alternatively, some groups go to EBC first, then divert south of Lobuche to Gokyo anti-clockwise.) Whatever your itinerary, be aware that EBC, Kala Pattar, the Cho La and Gokyo Ri are all at very high altitude (5300-5500 m) and to reach all four over a period of 4-6 days demands that you are thoroughly acclimatised first.

Your choice of itinerary should be influenced by factors listed below: think about these, and discuss them with any travelling companions:

- your level of experience and confidence at trekking
- your previous experience at altitude, if any
- how long you have available
- your budget, not only for the package but also for local spending and tips.

Unless you've done this kind of trekking before, it's better to plan conservatively and within your capabilities. If you have a wonderful time, you could always return in future, but if you feel constantly under pressure, exhausted or unwell from altitude, it will spoil your holiday.

Choosing a tour operator

Although it's perfectly possible, and may be preferable for some, to make all your own arrangements and trek independently, this book is written main for those who use a tour operator. Once you have decided which trek you want, consider other factors before choosing. Read online reviews, check websites and seek out personal recommendations. Assuming you have found one or more operators that seem to offer the trek you want at a price you can afford, consider also the following:

- Exactly what is and is not included in the price? See our table on page 26.
- What is their policy on porter protection, and do they advise on tipping?
- How long have they been operating treks in Nepal and what has been their response to the 2015 earthquake?
- How well does their guidance reflect environmental awareness?
- What fallback options may be offered should illness or accident strike?

If you are unsure about how you will cope with altitude, the choice of itinerary becomes very important: some tour operators will offer a less demanding alternative to clients who are taken ill, others may expect you to stay put and await the group's return, or even treat your holiday as over and return you to Kathmandu.

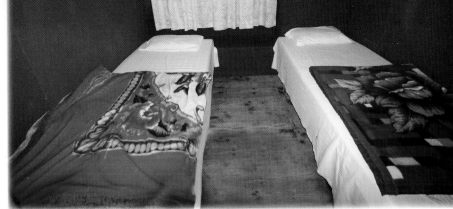
Typical twin-bedded room: basic but clean

Teahouse trekking

This book assumes that you intend to overnight and eat meals in the many teahouses or lodges that line the main trekking routes, although if you wish to overnight at EBC you will be camping in tents. Some teahouses are small family homes with a couple of rooms partitioned for trekkers, indeed in some villages nearly all the homes have been converted. Others are huge, purpose-built guest houses, almost hotels, sometimes dominated by large groups.

The facilities you can expect vary widely. Your Nepali hosts may or may not still live in their home, but often it is family members and friends who are doing the cooking and serving the meals. The welcome is usually warm, but people are working really hard and have few, if any, labour-saving devices.

Tour operators will brief you about what to expect, and some may offer an option for 'luxury' trekking. The golden rule is to beware of making assumptions. Rooms with two single beds are common, but the 'walls' may consist of plywood panels, so although you have privacy, don't expect sound-proofing. The door may have a padlock, but the room won't have a power socket, nor plumbing, nor will it be heated. Although it should have electric lighting, this may be very dim so if you want to read in bed, use your headtorch.

Electricity supplies are unlikely to be 100% reliable and services such as recharging phones and batteries come at a price. If wifi is available, it may be charged for, and in all cases, the higher the altitude, the higher the prices. (This applies to internet cafés, the price of beer and soft drinks and most other things.) Although by western standards all these charges are quite modest, you may have concerns about leaving your precious smartphone or irreplaceable camera battery in a public place for hours on end while it charges. We suggest you take at least two spare batteries for your camera, and perhaps also a solar charger.

There should be running water but hot water often relies on solar panels and may run tepid or cold. Hot (or warm) showers are usually available at extra cost. Toilets will be inside the lodges, and at lower altitudes will be western-style flush toilets. Meals will be served in a large communal area which typically has tables and benches or chairs arranged around a central stove which may burn dried yak dung. Hot drinks are generally served after meals, and some lodges have ultraviolet water filtration systems.

Fitness, exercise and heart rate

Thorough preparation before you go is important. Muscles get stronger if they are used regularly, at a suitable level and for a sustained period. This is known as the training effect. As a walker, you might think the most important muscles to train are in your legs, but in fact your lungs and heart are even more vital.

If you train your heart muscle, it pumps blood more efficiently and delivers more oxygen. Cardiovascular (CV) fitness refers to how well your heart and lungs work together. You will improve your CV fitness by taking sustained exercise several times a week, strenuous enough to keeps your heart rate in your target zone.

Your target zone

This table shows target zone heart rates by age bands: these are calculated from a crude formula (70-80% of estimated maximum heart rate) that makes no allowance for individual differences or fitness level. The result is targets that are very conservative, especially for mature, fit people. Ideally, you should measure your existing fitness level: take your pulse before getting out of bed to find your resting heart rate (RHR). As you become fitter, your RHR should reduce because a fitter heart pumps more blood per beat. Your RHR also lets you calculate your individual target zone. Details of this method are given on our website: *www.rucsacs.com/links/tte*.

Exercising above your target zone will not increase your CV fitness significantly, and may tire you faster. Exercising below it will benefit you in weight loss, increasing your power-to-weight ratio, but it will not noticeably improve your fitness level.

If you exercise within your target zone for 20-40 minutes every other day, within a few weeks you will notice your fitness level rising, and your RHR falling. You will have to work harder to push your heart rate into the target zone, and it will return to normal faster whenever you slow down. The guideline is to work hard enough to make you pant, but not so hard that you cannot also talk. A wrist-worn heart rate monitor takes out the guesswork by showing you a continuous read-out.

A fit person ascends more easily, using less oxygen per unit of work done. When everything takes more effort than usual, as at altitude, it helps if your heart is pumping the available oxygen to your muscles and brain efficiently.

How your target zone varies with your age

Age range (years)	Target zone (beats per minute)
16 – 20	140 – 170
21 – 25	136 – 166
26 – 30	133 – 162
31 – 35	130 – 157
36 – 40	126 – 153
41 – 45	122 – 149
46 – 50	119 – 144
51 – 55	116 – 140
56 – 60	112 – 136
61 – 65	108 – 132
66 – 70	105 – 128
71 – 75	102 – 123
76 – 80	98 – 119

If you need to lose weight, do so well before your trip, and do it gradually. Carrying surplus fat adds to your baggage and makes trekking more of an effort. It is also a risk factor in altitude illness. However, don't go to extremes: fat insulates your body from cold, and if you are very thin, you will need more clothing to avoid hypothermia, especially at night.

Where and how to exercise

The answer depends on your preference, your lifestyle and where you live. If you live in or near pleasant terrain for walking/jogging, have considerable self-discipline and don't mind the weather, suitable footwear may be all you need. Consider getting a device with a heart rate monitor to make your training more systematic. Try going out with a friend who also wants to get fit: if your training needs and paces are compatible, you will motivate each other.

If brisk walking and jogging do not appeal, find a mix of activities that you enjoy and can do often enough (three times per week). If you dislike an activity, you won't stick to it. Anything that puts your heart rate into the target zone is fine, e.g. energetic dancing, cycling or swimming. Consider joining a gym or fitness centre, as their equipment is designed to measure and build CV fitness. A gym makes you independent of the weather and hours of daylight, there are trained staff, and it's easy to monitor your progress.

Avoid relying on a single form of exercise. The smooth surface of a treadmill does nothing to prepare your leg muscles for rough terrain or steep descents. If you use a gym for convenience, try to complement it with some hill-walking in the weeks prior to departure, preferably on consecutive days and with steep ascents and descents.

However you exercise, minimise the risk of straining your body, especially at first, by warming up slowly beforehand, cooling down afterwards, and stretching both before and after. Stretch beforehand to reduce the risk of injury, but make sure your muscles are warm before you stretch. Stretch after exercise to prevent a build-up of lactic acid in your muscles, which leads to stiffness the next day. Take a water container and drink plenty before, during and after your sessions.

When and how often to exercise

You don't have to become an exercise junkie to trek to Everest, nor give up your normal pleasures, but if you are fit you will enjoy the experience more. Start training long before you go: if you are very unfit, aim to start three to six months in advance. If you smoke, give it up at least until after your trip.

For CV fitness, you need at least 20-minute sessions to achieve a training effect, but build up to 30 minutes, and, approaching your departure date, 40-60 minutes. Better still, spend some time walking fast on rough or hilly terrain to prepare your body for consecutive days of sustained effort at altitude.

The best frequency for training is every other day: the body needs a rest day to extract maximum benefit from the training session. Since you may miss the odd session, three times per week is the goal for your main training period. Prior to departure, build up to longer sessions with higher target heart rates.

11

Altitude effects

This section explains the cause of altitude problems and how to prevent or minimise them. We have tried to summarise the relevant bits of a large technical literature, using a minimum of medical jargon, focusing on practical advice and drawing on experience gained at first hand. For more detail, please consult one of the many books or websites written by experts on high-altitude medicine.

How your body responds to lack of oxygen

The problem for your body at altitude is the shortage of oxygen. As you climb higher, the air gets thinner. At Everest Base Camp (EBC), altitude 5360 m/17,590 ft, the atmosphere holds less than half the oxygen than at sea level. So your heart and lungs have to work more than twice as hard to maintain oxygen supply to your vital organs. (At the summit of Everest, there is about 33% of the oxygen at sea level, so climbers descending to EBC find the air there oxygen-rich by comparison.)

Your heart is the pump that makes your blood circulate. The lungs load the vital oxygen into your red blood cells for delivery to your tissues (muscles, brain and other organs). The demand from your muscles depends on their activity level, but your brain needs a surprising amount of oxygen (15% of your body's total demand). If your brain lacks oxygen, your judgement declines, movement control suffers and speech become confused.

Your body responds to needing more oxygen in various ways:
* you breathe faster and deeper
* your heart beats faster, increasing the oxygen circulating to your tissues and forcing blood into parts of your lungs which aren't normally used
* your body gets rid of excess fluid, making the blood thicker, and eventually it creates more red blood cells.

Red blood cells (greatly magnified)

The timescale of these responses varies: you start to breathe faster right away, and your heart rate rises within minutes. It can take several days before your blood starts to thicken: if you notice that you are urinating a lot, that is probably a sign that your body is acclimatising. Making more red blood cells is a much longer process, taking a week or more: it is important that your itinerary allows enough time for this to get under way.

At altitude, breathe deeply and freely as far as possible. Sleep is important for the body's adjustment. Avoid sleeping pills and alcohol, both of which depress breathing while asleep. Allow digestion time after your evening meal before going to sleep.

Be aware of other effects of altitude. Some people (especially women) experience swollen hands, face and ankles, so remove any tight-fitting jewellery before going to altitude. Contact lens wearers may find that the lenses become painful to wear at altitude, and should take spectacles as an alternative. Many people find they make more intestinal gas at altitude, but this is harmless unless your companions lack a sense of humour.

Acute Mountain Sickness (AMS)

Acute Mountain Sickness is what medical people call altitude sickness. 'Acute' here means that the onset is sudden, not that you will be acutely ill. This section helps you to decide whether your symptoms are mild, moderate or severe. Mild or moderate symptoms often disappear if you rest and ascend no further, but severe symptoms demand *immediate* descent, even at night. If you ignore the symptoms and behave unwisely, you may become seriously ill.

Individuals vary widely in how they respond to altitude, so you need to take responsibility for monitoring your own condition. Age and gender affect your response. At moderate altitude, young people are more likely to suffer AMS than their elders, and the risk decreases with age in a linear trend. Gender effects are more complicated: females are more susceptible to AMS, but less likely to develop its complications. Doctors can't fully explain the variability, and it is certain that there are genetic factors at work.

Mild AMS can affect you at any altitude above 2100 m (7000 feet), occasionally even lower. It feels like a hangover and usually starts with a headache (which should respond to pain relief) combined with one or more of the following:
- feeling sick
- lack of appetite
- sleeplessness
- feeling lousy, lacking energy.

Altitude has a dehydrating effect, and dehydration alone can cause headaches. So if you have a headache, first drink a litre of water, and perhaps take a mild painkiller (aspirin, paracetamol or ibuprofen). If the headache disappears and you have no other symptoms, your body was just reminding you to drink more fluid. Mild AMS is bearable, and if it goes away after a rest or a downhill stretch you will be able to continue your trek.

Moderate AMS is seriously unpleasant. It differs from mild in that:
• there is likely to be vomiting
• the headache does not respond to pain relief, and
• the victim may be very short of breath even when not exercising (e.g. after resting for 15 minutes).

Severe AMS can develop from moderate AMS if symptoms are ignored. It is very dangerous to ignore, or try to conceal, severe symptoms. These may include ataxia (loss of muscular co-ordination and balance), altered mental states such as confusion, aggression or withdrawal. Serious complications can follow, and if untreated, may lead to death.

However, severe AMS and complications are very unlikely on the trek to EBC if you follow a sensible itinerary and react appropriately to any warning signs. Take more seriously any symptoms that persist overnight. Your guide or tour leader should be alert to the acclimatisation of everybody in their group, and may be able to adjust the itinerary to suit individual needs. However, they can help you only if you communicate truthfully about how you are feeling. There is no stigma about having AMS: it can happen to the fittest of trekkers and mountaineers.

In essence, AMS is avoidable and treatable as follows:
• if you have symptoms, rest, drink fluids and don't ascend further.
• if you are getting worse, or have complications, descend at once.

The table below may help to work out how seriously to rate your symptoms:

AMS symptoms and points

symptom	points	symptom	points
headache	1	headache (resistant to painkillers)	2
insomnia	1	vomiting	2
nausea or loss of appetite	1	breathing difficulty at rest	3
dizziness	1	abnormal fatigue	3
		low urine production	3

Interpretation

total degree of AMS		treatment
1-3	mild	drink fluids, painkiller, rest
4-6	moderate	drink fluids, painkiller no more ascent until better
7+	severe	immediate descent

Diamox and other drugs

The medical research literature on drugs and altitude illness is extensive, and acetazolamide (trade name Diamox) has been studied for over 40 years. When you exert yourself at altitude, you pant, venting carbon dioxide; this can reduce the acidity of your blood. Diamox blocks or slows the enzymes involved in converting carbon dioxide, thereby stopping the blood from becoming too alkaline, and stimulating the rate and depth of breathing. As a result, it speeds up acclimatisation. Some people take Diamox with them because it can help in prevention, as well as treatment, of AMS.

In most countries, you need a doctor's prescription for Diamox, although it is widely sold in Kathmandu, Lukla and Namche Bazaar. Before rushing off to get a prescription, however, consider the possible downside. It can occasionally cause a severe allergic reaction. So if you plan to take it, try it out ahead of your trip to test if you are allergic, to experiment with dosage and to see whether you mind the side-effects. These include:

- increased flow of urine (diuresis)
- numbness or tingling in hands, feet and face
- nausea and/or bizarre dreams
- finding that carbonated drinks taste flat.

Since altitude has a diuretic effect anyway, many people prefer to avoid Diamox as it creates further interruptions to sleep in order to urinate. Some doctors say this is a problem of excess dosage. The recommended dosage used to be 250 mg three times a day, starting several days before ascending. Some authorities advise trying 125 mg daily at bedtime starting on the day before ascending, and increasing the dosage only if need be. Medical authorities tend to favour Diamox, especially for the minority who are unusually susceptible to altitude symptoms. However, most trekkers don't need it, and some who use it have symptoms regardless.

Ginkgo biloba is a herbal remedy that has been found helpful in preventing, but not treating, altitude illness: start taking it at sea level, ideally a few days in advance of travel. It is thought to stimulate better circulation. Many lodges and tea houses serve garlic soup as an aid to acclimatisation. Although there is no medical evidence to support it, the soup is a popular and a tasty way to increase your fluid intake.

Summary: how to prevent and manage AMS
- prepare well by improving your cardiovascular fitness
- drink plenty of fluids (two to four litres of water per day), plus fluids at meals
- avoid sleeping pills, excessive salt and alcohol
- eat small amounts of food often, even if you don't feel hungry
- if you have AMS symptoms, rest until you have recovered and do not ascend further.

Advice on food and drink

A diet rich in carbohydrates helps to prevent AMS symptoms, and you may find the traditional Nepali *dal bhat* (lentil stew with steamed rice) very suitable. Most of the places you stay will serve it among other local dishes and versions of pizza and pasta, but after a week or two, you may find the diet monotonous. Loss of appetite is a common side-effect of altitude, so bring some snacks such as dried fruit, trail mix, cereal bars or chocolate. They will boost your energy and morale, and can be shared with others. Many people suffer very dry throats and coughs at altitude, so consider taking throat and cough sweets.

Few people carry sufficient water, and even fewer keep it handy enough. You dehydrate quickly when walking at altitude: every time you breathe out, you lose moisture.

Also altitude has a diuretic effect, and especially when exercising you are continually losing water vapour as invisible sweat. Aim to drink two to four litres per day on top of the liquid you take with meals.

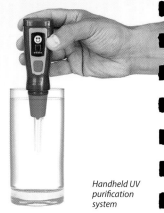

Try to drink before you become thirsty. A water bottle or bladder with tube is ideal as it lets you take sips whenever needed without having to stop or fiddle with rucksacks. Some lodges provide filtered water, others boiled; it is unwise to rely on buying water in disposable plastic water bottles both because it may not be available and because

Handheld UV purification system

of the litter and recycling problem that this creates. If in doubt, check the colour of your urine: if it's pale straw colour that's fine, but yellow warns that you are dehydrated.

Some lodges provide boiled water that is safe to drink. (At any altitude, boiling water even briefly makes it safe.) Take your own purification system as backup. Ultraviolet filtration systems can be handheld and claim to kill over 99.9% of bacteria and viruses. If using iodine drops or tablets, follow instructions about standing time and dosage in cold conditions. The flavour can be neutralised with Vitamin C tablets or fruit powder. (Iodine works better than chlorine because it protects you against giardia, and for short trips it is the preferred option.)

Help to limit fluid lost through sweating by adjusting your clothing. Try to anticipate your body's heat production. Shed excess layer(s) before you start to overheat, and restore them just before you start to chill (e.g. for a rest stop or when the weather changes). Because each of these actions means stopping and fiddling with your rucksack, you may find it easier to keep a steady pace and wear clothes designed for flexibility. For example, jackets should have underarm zippers and pockets large enough to hold gloves and hat.

At altitude, take care to avoid your water bottle or bladder freezing during the night, if need be by keeping it well wrapped or warmed by your body heat.

Communal eating in a teahouse

Other health and safety issues

If you consult your doctor before booking, take the altitude information with you. Unless your medical history includes serious risk factors, sound preparation for the trek should have healthy side-effects. Check which vaccinations are required and recommended for Nepal, and what is the timetable. Take advice about anti-malarial drugs and insect repellents and follow it carefully. Malaria is a life-threatening disease which is easy to prevent but difficult to treat. If you're spending time at lower altitudes you may need protection.

Your feet are about to become the most important part of your body, so consider seeing a foot specialist and try to toughen up your feet before you go. Blood donors should allow at least eight to ten weeks after donation before departure. Remember to visit your dentist well in advance.

Many visitors have digestive upsets in Nepal, because their systems can't cope with contaminated food and water. Simple precautions reduce the chances of such trouble. You may have heard 'cook it, peel it, wash it, or forget it' – sound advice, but not sufficient. Beware of reheated dishes, blended drinks, undercooked meat, ice-cream products and ice: freezing doesn't kill micro-organisms. Food that is thoroughly cooked and served immediately should be safe.

Keeping yourself clean while on trek isn't always easy: be scrupulous about cleaning your hands before touching food or cutlery. Antibacterial gel makes for less litter than wet wipes, but both are very useful.

Anything destined for your mouth (toothbrush or food) needs to be washed in safe drinking water. Just in case, take along anti-diarrhoea medicine. Bowel paralysers containing loperamide relieve symptoms and help you to sustain your hike. Rehydration salts can restore your fluid balance faster than plain water. Most diarrhoea clears up within a few days, but be sure to drink plenty of fluids, and if problems persist, seek medical advice.

Most Nepali plumbing can't cope with toilet paper: don't try to flush it away, even in city hotels, but use the bin provided. If this seemss unhygienic, think about the effects of a blocked toilet. Depending on the location and altitude, toilets may be western-style flush toilets or squat-holes, with or without a platform for your feet.

At altitude, the sun's rays are far stronger, because the thinner air filters out less of the harmful radiation. Since the sun is already strong, the risk of sunburn is doubly severe. Take a wide-brimmed hat to protect your face and the back of your neck, and use cream with a high Sun Protection Factor (ideally SPF 50-60).

While on trek, be alert for yak trains. Listen for yak bells or the herders' shouts, and be ready to pass the word forward or back, to warn other trekkers. Yaks, especially when laden, are large, heavy animals. They are also easily panicked. Protect yourself, as well as them, by giving them plenty of space. Never embark on a bridge if yaks are approaching. On the trail, step aside well ahead of time, moving uphill for a few metres, then stand still and stay alert until they have passed.

Equipment and packing

For trekking, the most important items are comfortable, well-tested hiking boots, a suitable rucksack (daypack) and kit bag (baggage), and good sleeping gear for cold nights in lodges and teahouses. Your daypack should have at least 30 litres capacity, so there's plenty of room for spare clothing, drinking water and other essentials. If in doubt, err on the large side for easier retrieval and packing. Your main kit bag will be carried by porters or loaded on yaks, so it should be large, soft and light, without a frame, wheels or dangling straps. Large rucksacks and suitcases are not suitable. Your tour operator may provide a bag, but if not seek something waterproof, such as a sailing bag or sports holdall with waterproof liner.

A liner keeps your main sleeping bag clean: use microfleece for extra warmth, or silk for its tiny size and luxurious feel. Some people like to use a sleeping mat on top of the mattresses in lodges, for reasons of fragrance or hygiene. And although pillows are provided, you may prefer to use your own pillowcase. If you are camping, for example at EBC, then a good quality sleeping mat is essential for warmth.

Another item to consider is trekking poles. They improve your balance, save effort and reduce knee strain, especially on steep descents. A pair is better than only one for balance and efficiency, but some people prefer to keep their hands free. It is therefore useful if your daypack has loops to let you stow the pole(s).

Before you pack for Nepal, consider your kit in two categories: stuff you can leave behind in Kathmandu and stuff you need while trekking. The latter comprises heavy stuff for your main kit bag and much less for your daypack. Long before you depart for Nepal, do a trial pack to find out if you are within target weight for the Lukla flight: weight limits on this flight are very strict, typically 15 kg/33 lb. Leave out your hiking boots, and anything else you will be wearing on the flight.

Pack in your hand baggage anything fragile (torches, sunglasses, camera) and any vital medicines, as well as travel documents, ticket, vaccination records and other valuables. Ensure that any sharp objects are packed as hold baggage. Take care over packaging: clear polythene zip-lock bags are great for keeping small stuff handy and visible, and cling-film helps to keep moisture off batteries and delicate items.

Kit bags being weighed at Lukla airport

Packing checklist

The list below is divided into essential and desirable. Experienced hikers may disagree about what belongs in each category, but this is a starting point. You won't have access to your kit bag all day, so carry in your daypack everything you need for each day's walk, including spare clothing, blister protection, plenty of water and any snacks or medicines you need.

Essential

- well broken-in walking boots
- plenty of specialist walking socks
- comfortable, lightweight daypack (small rucksack)
- many layers of suitably warm clothing, including thermal underwear
- hat(s) and balaclava for sun and wind protection
- sun protection for eyes and face (good quality sunglasses, high SPF suncream)
- gloves, glove liners and/or warm mittens
- waterproof, breathable jacket and trousers
- water carrier(s) and water purification system e.g. tablets, drops or UV)
- first aid kit, including blister, headache and diarrhoea relief
- toilet tissue (biodegradable)
- antibacterial gel and wet wipes
- small bags for litter disposal
- wash bag with all you need for cleaning skin and teeth
- trekking towel
- headtorch, plus pocket torch as backup, and spare batteries
- warm sleeping bag, perhaps with liner
- sleeping mat (essential only if camping)
- enough cash for tips for guides, cooks and porters, plus other holiday spending; take plenty of small notes.

Desirable

- trekking pole(s)
- light and rugged camera and charger; take several spare batteries and memory cards
- binoculars
- pouch or secure pockets: to keep small items handy but safe
- snacks and throat sweets
- thermal liner (if in doubt about your sleeping bag)
- pillowcase or inflatable pillow
- ear plugs (if you are a light sleeper)
- spare shoes (eg trainers or crocs), spare bootlaces
- notebook and pen, playing cards, music player and book for down time
- guidebook.

Loading the yaks on trek

2·1 Background information : Nepal
Geography and wildlife

Nepal claims about one third of the entire Himalayan range. Almost rectangular, the country is slightly larger in area than New York State or England, with a population of about 28 million people. It extends 800 km from India's Uttaranchal region in the west to its Sikkim region in the east, and 200 km from the Ganges plain in the south to the Tibetan plateau in the north. Yet in a short northward journey from India to the Great Himalaya on the Tibet border, Nepal presents a series of east-west climatic bands that together display some of the broadest diversities of altitude, flora, and fauna in the world.

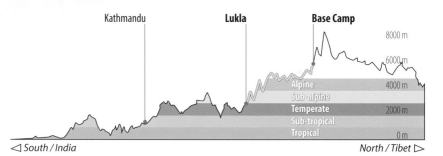

Kathmandu   **Lukla**   **Base Camp**

8000 m
6000 m
Alpine   4000 m
Sub-alpine
Temperate   2000 m
Sub-tropical
Tropical   0 m

◁ South / India   North / Tibet ▷

Nepal's tropical zone extends from near sea level in India, to the foothills of the Mahabharat Hills 30 km further north. The climate is warm and humid: mango, papaya and banana thrive, with other fruit growing higher up.

The next band is the sub-tropical zone in which Kathmandu is sited. It ranges in altitude from 1000 to 2000 m. Crops include potato, wheat, rice and citrus fruits. Oak and rhododendron also flourish.

Rhododendron

The next 50 km straddles the Lesser Himalaya temperate zone, at altitudes of 2000 to 3000 m, just including Lukla (2840 m).

Pine forest

Ripening papayas

Oak thrives here, together with birch, juniper, blue pine, fir, bamboo, rhododendron and laurel. Although slopes are steep and frost possible for half the year, crops such as potato, wheat, rice, and barley are grown.

Between 3000-4000 m in altitude, the zone is sub-alpine: in summer, potato and other crops barely survive and sheep, goats and yaks are out to pasture. Birch, juniper, fir and rhododendron survive, but becoming ever smaller at higher altitudes.

Above 4000 m is the alpine zone where, beyond the tree-line, the vegetation is mainly scrub rhododendron, juniper and barberry – eventually giving way to herbs, grasses and sedges. Above 5000 m, there is no vegetation and virtually no human habitation – an exception being Gorak Shep, at 5140 m.

The Greater Himalaya rise within a narrow belt. In Sanskrit, Himalaya means 'land of snows', and it includes eight of the world's ten highest peaks: Everest, Kanchenjunga, Lhotse, Makalu, Cho Oyu, Dhaulagiri I, Manaslu and Annapurna I. Much of the Khumbu valley and Sagarmāthā National Park – through which the trails to Everest pass – lie within this Greater Himalaya region.

Khumbu icefall

Yak

As well as creating a vast diversity of ecology and flora, these mountain ranges also fundamentally influence the climates across the entire subcontinent. The mountains shelter the plains of India from the cold, dry winds from the north and promote more luxuriant vegetation there. They also block the passage of the monsoons northwards and so contribute to the dryness of the Tibetan plateau, and the Taklamakan and Gobi deserts.

Fast-flowing river, Khumbu valley

Nepal's rivers have a huge impact locally and regionally. Their valleys, passes and gorges have always offered routes through the Himalaya for trade and migration; their phenomenal depth and beauty attracts tourism (by some reckoning the Kali Gandaki Gorge is the deepest in the world); and the huge volumes of water that they disgorge not only irrigate communities to the south but can also flood them.

Since the 1970s, Nepal has actively protected its fauna. In support of this aim it has established eight national parks including Langtang and Sagarmāthā, four conservation areas including Mustang and Annapurna, and three wildlife reserves. Several of its mammals are notable for their rarity: red panda, snow leopard, clouded leopard, Tibetan fox, Tibetan wolf, Bengal fox and Bengal tiger. Nepal has 27 Important Bird Areas, home to a wide variety of species, including 36 globally threatened ones such as certain vultures, eagles and pheasants. Native reptiles include the pit viper and monitor lizard.

On the trail, however, you will see sheep, cattle and goats (domestic and wild), together with beasts of burden such as donkeys, mules, horses and yaks. The typical 'yak' is actually a hybrid: when cross-bred with cattle, yaks become stronger and more manageable, and can thrive at lower altitudes. Strictly speaking, a hybrid is known as a *dzo* (male, and sterile) or a *dzomo* (female, and fertile), but most people just call them all yaks.

Yak carrying trekkers' bags

Geology, earthquakes and glaciers

Earthquake damage to village house

The Himalaya and the land-mass of Nepal were formed about 50 million years ago when the Indian tectonic plate was driven northward towards Eurasia. During this process, three things happened to the oceanic crust between the continents. First, most of the crust was thrust underneath the Eurasian plate, where frictional forces triggered volcanic activity. Second, some of the top surface of the oceanic plate was piled up into a wedge at the edge of the Eurasian plate, wrinkled like butter in front of an advancing knife. Finally, continued pressure from the Indian plate compressed that wedge into mountainous folds that became the Himalaya. This geological origin has three implications:

• The rocks of the region are a mixture of sedimentary (sea-deposited), igneous (volcanic), and metamorphic (altered by heat or pressure).

• The highest peaks, where they have not been completely eroded by wind and ice, contain uplifted sedimentary materials in many places – there are fossils from the ocean floor atop Mount Everest.

• The Himalaya lie on a multitude of active fault lines, along which earthquakes are inevitable.

On 25 April 2015 a massive earthquake (Richter 7.8) hit the country, killing about 9000 people, destroying half a million houses, leaving more than a million people in need of food and triggering an avalanche on Mount Everest. There were over 100 aftershocks, of which the 12 May quake (Richter 7.3) was unusually destructive, causing over 200 deaths, and injuries to over 2500 people. This was a double blow to the Nepali people who had already started the rebuilding effort. Even when emergency supplies were available, there were huge challenges in getting help to villages made inaccessible by the destruction of roads and tracks.

Nepal is no stranger to earthquakes. During the 20th century, it suffered five substantial quakes, with loss of life ranging from 80 to 8000 and with grim social consequences. In a country where GDP averages a mere $700 per person, the prospect of having to rebuild the family home – let alone other infrastructure – is overwhelming. Aid is vital for the rebuilding effort. But it is also crucial for mitigating the less visible disasters: dealing with the mental stress and illness that follow in the wake of such devastation; and helping families to cope with the pressure on their men to work abroad on construction sites in the Gulf.

Long after the media attention has died down and the major donations of foreign aid start to be distributed, continuing income from tourism and trekking will play a vital role in bringing in resources for rebuilding. As individuals, we can help not only by donating, but also by continuing to visit Nepal for trekking, thus helping the people of Kathmandu and the mountains to earn vital funds.

Glaciers have as great an impact on Nepal's geography as earthquakes. Much of the Himalaya's cragginess is due to glaciation. Glaciers start above the line of perpetual snow, where ice accumulates into sheets. Where the sheets are thick enough, pressure causes melting where they meet the underlying rock. Meltwater lubricates the glacier so it slides gently downhill. These points of contact undergo both freezing and thawing, causing erosion by 'plucking' of the rockface and scraping by the embedded material. The plucked rocks eventually become *moraines* – lines of rocks running down the sides or middle of the glacier, or deposited at its end.

At lower elevations, the glaciers become rivers. The Khumbu is home to many rivers, which are part of the Sun Kosi river system. Much of the trek from Lukla to Everest Base Camp follows the Dudh Kosi river, which eventually feeds the Ganges.

Geological features to notice include:

- granite, e.g. the large vertical rockface just after Monjo, to the left of steep steps moraines, from Lobuche upward

- mountain folding, e.g. on your left halfway from Lobuche to Gorak Shep

- glacial lakes at Gokyo, and the flat dry lake bed at Gorak Shep

- seracs of the Khumbu icefall, near Base Camp, where the glacier speeds up over steep ground.

Glacier near Everest Base Camp

History and economy

Parts of Nepal have been inhabited for over 10,000 years, but the first recorded civilisation was that of the Kiranti. Probably from Tibet, they arrived in the Kathmandu valley, extended their influence and thrived for 1200 years until AD 300. Other long-running dynasties followed, though the region eventually fragmented into dozens of rival kingdoms. In the 18th century, the Gurkha Shah family assumed power, re-unified the region and confirmed Kathmandu as its capital. But by the 19th century, the powerful Rana clan had taken control, keeping the Shahs as puppet rulers.

In parallel, the British East India Company had extended its reach from India, culminating in 1816 in the Treaty of Segauli. This treaty established the borders between India and Nepal and paved the way for friendship between Britain and Nepal, mutual understanding, and respect for each other's national interests. During this period the Gurkhas (from western Nepal) first enlisted in the British Army.

In 1923, Britain and Nepal formally signed a Treaty of Friendship that helped to define Nepal as a sovereign country. Nepal finally became a democratic regime after a revolution in 1951. Subsequent decades have seen turbulent periods of royal coups, multi-party politics, royal familicide and civil war. A new constitution was finally launched in 2015.

Modern Nepal has an unusual mixed economy. Agriculture accounts for 81% of employment but only 33% of GDP; services account for 16% and 50% respectively; and industry for only 3% and 17% respectively. India is Nepal's largest trading partner, responsible for half of its exports and over 80% of its imports. Remittances from Nepalese workers overseas form a major part of the country's revenue.

Agriculture is Nepal's main source of employment

Practical information for visitors

Arrival

Most trekkers arrive at Tribhuvan International Airport, Kathmandu (KTM). After passing through customs, the main hall offers tourist information, hotel reservations and pre-paid taxi vouchers (in 2016 about £6 for the 20-minute ride to central Kathmandu). However, if you are on a guided tour you will probably be met at the airport.

Currency and how much you need

Nepal's currency is rupees (NPR) and as of 2016 there were about 150 NPR to the pound sterling (over 100 per US dollar). You can exchange currency at the airport, but there are many more money changers in Kathmandu. In touristy places, US dollar notes may be accepted, and perhaps also euros, but you need plenty of rupees while on trek. It's always useful to have US dollars in small denominations, and credit/debit cards as backup.

How much you need while on trek depends on what your prepaid tour already includes: check this against the table below. It also depends on how many soft drinks and snacks you buy, whether you purify your own water, and how often you take showers and charge batteries. Remember that prices increase with altitude: for example, in 2015 a Snickers bar cost $5 at Gorak Shep. When having meals out, expect to pay 23% above the menu prices (13% VAT and 10% service charge).

Typically included	Sometimes included	Usually excluded
Return flight to Lukla and other transfers within Nepal	International flight	Travel insurance (obligatory)
Sagarmatha Park permit and trek registration	Sightseeing trips from Kathmandu	Nepal visa
Hotel in Kathmandu and accommodation on trek	Meals in Kathmandu	Hot showers, drinks, wifi and battery charging while on trek
Services of the tour leader, guides, porters	Meals on trek	Tips for trekking staff (obligatory)

Tipping the team

Tips are normally given on the last trekking day, sometimes as part of a ceremony. When you see how hard the team work, and realise how low their wages are, you will understand why we say that tipping is obligatory. If your tour operator provides guidance, follow it: they may operate a pooled system, and everybody benefits from some degree of consistency. In case you are trekking in a small group, here is a rough rule of thumb: budget about one day's pay per team member per seven days' trekking. For example, if the guide is paid $25 per day and a porter $15, then appropriate tips for a 7-day trek would be $25 and $15 respectively, and for a 14-day trek double that.

Pay the tips in rupees if possible, but if you have run low it's better to tip generously in dollars or sterling, or even a mixture, than to tip meanly. (The guide is less likely to have trouble getting a fair rate of exchange than the porters.) It's fine to buy drinks and snacks for team members while on trek, and to donate suitable items of clothing or equipment at the end, but don't reduce your tip on either account. Nepalis can't pay their children's school fees with used clothing, they need cash.

Travel insurance

Take out suitable travel insurance as soon as you book, otherwise you won't be covered in the event of cancellation. Check that the policy includes trekking at altitudes over 5000 m. In insurance terms, every route in this book is hiking at altitude, not mountaineering – the latter involves the use of equipment such as crampons and jumars. If you have an annual inclusive policy, check if they have a lower altitude limit: it is much cheaper to pay a small supplement than to take out another policy.

It is obvious, but worth repeating, that the 24-hour phone number for your policy must be easily found in an emergency. Carry at least two copies while in Nepal, one with your travel documents and another in your wallet or rucksack.

Time zones

Nepal is on Greenwich Mean Time +5 hr 45 minutes, so it's nearly 10 hours ahead of New York and nearly 14 hours ahead of Los Angeles. Should you plan to visit Tibet, note that it operates on Beijing time, which is GMT+8: the 2 hr 15 minute difference when crossing the border creates scope for confusion.

Power supply and telephoning

Electricity in Nepal is nominally 220v, 50Hz, but voltage can fluctuate and the supply often interrupted. Plugs are generally round-pin, but may have two or three pins. While on trek, expect to pay to recharge batteries, at prices that increase with altitude. You should carry voltage converters (if your appliances need 110v) and plug adaptors.

To dial Nepal from another country, dial the international access code (usually 00 but 011 from the US) then 977 for Nepal, followed by the rest of the number. To phone home from Nepal, the international access code is 00, followed by your country code (e.g. 44 for the UK or 1 for North America), then the rest of the number.

Using your mobile (cellphone) in Nepal could be very expensive unless you buy a Nepali SIM card, which makes it cheap, much cheaper than at home for most people. Rates from internet phone cafés in Thamel are very low; prices increase with altitude.

Local names, spellings and Mount Everest

In Nepal, villages, mountains and rivers are spelled in a variety of ways on maps, local signs and in guidebooks. We have adopted widely accepted spellings, but do not claim them as definitive. Be aware that Hs and Ys may come and go, CHs are sometime replaced by Js, and Ds by Ts. Tengboche and Thyangboche are the same place, and Awi Peak and Arakam Tse refer to the same mountain.

The mountain that westerners have since 1865 called Everest (after Sir George Everest, former British Surveyor-General of India) is properly known in Nepal as Sagarmāthā ('head/forehead above the sky') and in Tibet as Chomolungma ('holy mother of the gods'). We have reservations about the imported, colonial-era name for this mountain. However, to call it Sagarmāthā/Chomolungma throughout the book would have been unwieldy, even if politically more correct.

2·2 Kathmandu and beyond

Kathmandu offers a huge variety of hotels; the budget and mid-price ones are mainly in Thamel – the teeming heart of Kathmandu near the Royal Palace. Although only 1 km square, this lively district in the north-west of the city packs in 2500 businesses, including lots of restaurants and hotels. Some people prefer to stay in Patan, which lies about 10 km south of Thamel, south of the Bagmati River. Its main heritage attraction is Durbar Square, not to be confused with Kathmandu's Durbar Square.

Kathmandu – main sights

Boudhanath stands east of Thamel (about 30 minutes by taxi), just north of the airport. One of the world's largest stupas, it is a focus for pilgrimage and meditation for Tibetan Buddhists and local Nepalis, and was recognised as a World Heritage site in 1979. Walk clockwise around it (about 150 m) and ask permission before photographing people.

Boudhanath, one of the world's largest stupas

Swayambhunath is a huge Buddhist temple set on a hill to the west of Thamel, and one of the oldest religious sites in Nepal, founded in the 7th century. Its Tibetan name probably means 'sublime trees', a reference to varieties of trees on its hill. It's known as the 'monkey temple' because it is overrun by monkeys that steal fearlessly from visitors. Renovated before the 2015 earthquake, the dome was re-gilded using 20 kg of gold. The main central structures still stand, but surrounding buildings have suffered severe damage. The site can still be visited: walking to it from Thamel takes about half an hour.

Tibetan monk in front of Boudhanath

Patan Durbar Square is a jewel of Newari architecture, a complex of ornately carved temples located at a crossroads used by early traders. Most of its buildings date from the 17th and 18th centuries. Tragically, the 2015 earthquake destroyed some of its palaces and temples, including the three-storied Kasthamandap temple – one of the largest and most famous pagodas in Nepal, after which Kathmandu was named.

Durbar Square, after earthquake damage

29

Fortunately, the excellent Patan Museum, housed in a royal palace built in 1734, suffered only minor damage in the 2015 earthquake. It houses a priceless collection of Hindu and Buddhist objects and sculptures, superbly displayed, and also hosts cultural events such as Jazzmandu concerts and photographic exhibitions: **www.patanmuseum.gov.np**.

Pashupatinath, on the eastern outskirts of Kathmandu, is one of Nepal's most sacred Hindu temples. It survived the 2015 earthquake unscathed. Dedicated to Shiva, it attracts large numbers of elderly Hindus. Non-Hindus may not enter the main temple, but may visit other buildings and see the holy *sadhus* performing remarkable feats. It lies about 15 minutes' taxi-ride from Thamel.

Hindu gods Shiva and Parvati, Patan Museum

The Garden of Dreams makes a beautiful tranquil visit, almost hidden but only a few minutes' walk from Thamel. It remains largely intact after the 2015 earthquake.

Beyond Kathmandu

Kathmandu is a superb base from which to explore the region more broadly, including:
• trekking in other areas of Nepal, e.g. the Annapurnas, Dhaulagiri and the Kali Gandaki Gorge, or the former kingdom of Mustang
• visiting other National Parks such as Langtang
• taking a sight-seeing flight to view 8000 m mountains
• paragliding high above Pokhara, with the majestic Annapurnas as a backdrop
• Flying from Kathmandu (with the appropriate Chinese visa) to visit Tibet including its capital, Lhasa, and perhaps onwards to Mount Kailash
• attempting (in sections or in full) the 4500 km of the Great Himalaya Trail from Nanga Parbat in Kashmir to Namche Barwa in Tibet: see page 78.

2·3 The Sherpa people

Although many non-Nepali people use the term *Sherpa* as if it were synonymous with 'porter', Sherpas are actually an ethnic group. There are over 100,000 Sherpas worldwide, and they dominate the Khumbu, where they number about 45,000. Originally from the eastern part of Tibet, they migrated over the high passes into Nepal in the 1600s. Their language is regarded as a dialect of Tibetan, and is much more commonly spoken than written. Most Sherpas also speak Nepali, and some speak English and other languages. Nowadays, however, most regular porters are not Sherpas; many are Rais, Chetris and Limbus, or from other non-Sherpa clans.

Way of life

A hardy mountain people, Sherpas live on the ridges and in the river valleys at the edge of the Greater Himalaya at altitudes of 3300 - 4400 m. Their houses are typically stone-built and of two storeys, and the furniture consists of benches rather than moveable items. The houses are usually grouped into small villages, often isolated, but there are a few larger settlements, notably Namche Bazaar with a population of well over 1500.

The Sherpas move their livestock seasonally: winter, from November to February, is too cold for herding or farming, so they

Nepali boy

move to lower altitudes where possible. At New Year in late February they return to higher pastures, and until May they till the land and sow crops. Harvesting is from September to early November, after the rainy season. Their staple food is *dal bhat* (lentils and steamed rice) and also potatoes.

Inside a modern Nepali home

Sherpas practise Tibetan Buddhism, although they have woven in many animist and shamanic elements, so that most mountains and larger caves represent deities. They live and work at altitude partly to be closer to the gods. Sherpas also have strong community ties and shared practices and rituals that include hospitality, certain rites of passage, importance of the local lama, and *shey-shey* – an insistence on giving even in the face of continued polite refusal. Universally the Sherpas are treasured for their amiability, faithfulness, honesty and non-violence. Rates of literacy and schooling are low and there are successful governmental and humanitarian efforts to increase them. They are better in the Khumbu than anywhere else in the country, thanks to Sir Edmund Hillary and the Himalayan Trust.

Sherpa is also often used as a surname – a tradition dating from when early census-takers used their ethnicity as a surname. Their first name is often the day of their birth: Nyima (Sunday), Dawa (Monday), Mingma (Tuesday), Lhakpa (Wednesday), Phurba (Thursday), Pasang (Friday), Pemba (Saturday).

Trekking and mountaineering

From the earliest days of Himalayan mountaineering, the Sherpas' mix of local knowledge and resilience has played a crucial role in both guiding and portering. Research has shown that their impressive physical performance at altitude is partly genetic (at least 10 genes are specifically adapted to altitude), partly due to conditioning from their habitual hard physical labour at altitude and partly due to more efficient foot placement, gait and posture. From the latter, trekkers can watch and learn.

Porter lifting an immense load

Because of the high value placed on them by westerners, Sherpas who can guide on Everest are by Nepali standards well-paid. At the price of long periods away from their families, they can bring significant amounts of money home. But the Everest climbing season is short, and at other times of year many go abroad to work in the Gulf region or in the Alps.

A Sherpa typically starts his career as a porter, progresses to assistant cook and/or assistant guide, and culminates as a chief guide or sirdar. (Most but not all porters are male.) It is a hard career, with a fatal avalanche or slip always a possibility. There are commercial pressures too, as local tour operators have tried to pile loads exceeding 60 kg onto Sherpa backs, paid limited wages, and often provided no technical or medical support – though conditions are gradually improving. Please check and question the credentials of any operator you deal with, and try to evaluate whether their practices are ethical. Tip generously; and if you donate suitable gear at the end of your trek, do this on top of tipping: see page 26.

2·4 Buddhism and its buildings

Most of the religious buildings encountered on the trek are Buddhist. This is because the population of the Khumbu area is mainly Sherpa, of Tibetan Buddhist faith. By contrast, of Nepalis overall, 81% are Hindu and only 9% Buddhist.

Buddhism

Gautama Buddha was born in Nepal, as Prince Siddhartha, in Lumbini in the south of the country. After his enlightenment in India, his teachings spread across Asia via many routes – entering Nepal both from India to the south and thence reaching Kathmandu; and via Tibet from the north, carried and reinforced by the Sherpa people.

Buddhism is a path of spiritual development leading to insight into the true nature of reality. It teaches meditation and other practices as ways to develop the qualities of awareness, kindness, and wisdom, and ultimately to become enlightened and break the cycle of rebirth. Its Four Noble Truths hold that

All life involves suffering.

Suffering derives from craving.

Craving can be stopped.

In order to stop craving, follow the Noble Eightfold Path of right understanding, thought, conduct etc.

Stupas below Tengboche

Tibetan Buddhism – the basis of the Sherpa religion – places special emphasis on the status of the teacher (lama) and monastery; the relationship between life and death; certain rituals; and vivid symbolism. The Sherpa religion also combines shamanic and animist elements from earlier faiths including the widespread belief in gods-of-place. For example Mount Everest represents Chomolungma, the Mother of the Gods.

Inside the monastery at Tengboche

Sacred buildings

The trek to Everest passes significant Buddhist monasteries at Namche Bazaar, Tengboche, Deboche, Pangboche and Phortse, and Kathmandu has the Boudhanath and Swayambhunath temples.

Monasteries (or *gompas* from the Tibetan meaning 'remote location') are places of Buddhist learning and meditation. Their floorplan is typically based on a *mandala* – a sacred geometric design that represents the cosmos and the workings of divine powers. This layout includes a central prayer hall containing a *thangka* (large instructional painting often on silk), religious statues, benches for the monks or nuns, and adjacent accommodation. Nearby may be one or more *stupas* (also known as *chortens*). These are stone shrines with Buddha eyes on four sides to ward off evil spirits in all directions. They contain prayer books and relics of important lamas. Gompas are often attached to a private chapel (*lhang*) that has mural-painted walls, statues and books. The entrance to a monastery is guarded by a small gateway (*kani*). Its walls and ceiling are usually painted with protective religious figures.

A recurring image in Tibetan Buddhism is the Wheel of Life. Said to have been invented by Buddha himself, it is a teaching aid that represents the workings of such elements as the three poisons of ignorance, attachment and aversion; karma; and ways to escape from cyclical rebirth.

Other expressions of Buddhism

Beyond the sacred architecture of Buddhism, look out for *mani* stones – boulders or walls bearing prayers normally written in Tibetan script – often *Om mani padme hum* ('Hail to the jewel in the lotus'). They are often located on the trail near villages or monasteries. Respect your hosts: always keep the stone on your right as you pass it (a good-fortune, clockwise, circumambulation as seen from above), and never lean against it.

Mani stone below Phakding

Near monasteries you will see prayer wheels (aka *mani*-wheels). Mantras written on paper are held inside these cylinders. When you spin the cylinders (clockwise, as seen from above) the mantra will pass in front of you: again, pay respect by concentrating while you spin it, avoiding idle chatter.

Fluttering prayer flags are a ubiquitous and memorable feature of trekking in Nepal. They were developed under Buddhism in Tibet. Note that each colour has a meaning and always appears in the same sequence:
Blue – space
White – air (or cloud or wind)
Red – fire
Green – water
Yellow – earth

Prayer wheel above Lukla

2·5 Climbing Mount Everest

Context and first ascent

On a British-led expedition in 1953, Edmund Hillary (a New Zealander) and Tenzing Norgay (a Sherpa) achieved the first confirmed ascent of Mount Everest (8848 m).

Until the early 19th century, the volcano Chimborazo (Ecuador) had been thought the highest peak in the world. In 1852 the Great Trigonometric Survey of India determined that Mount Everest deserved this title, standing over 2500 m taller than Chimborazo. But the kingdoms of Tibet and Nepal both refused access to foreigners until Tibet eventually opened its borders in 1921.

Across the Himalaya, the Germans were focussing on climbing Nanga Parbat, the Italians on K2, and the French on Annapurna. That left Everest for the British. After several prior visits, Mallory and Irvine made their ill-fated attempt in 1924 from the north (Tibet). Throughout the 1930s, many expeditions were unsuccessful. When Nepal opened its borders in 1950, the technically easier southern approach to Everest became possible. After meticulous reconnaissance and planning, and making more use of oxygen and high-altitude porters than previously, the team effort finally succeeded, and on 29 May, Hillary and Tenzing summitted together.

Subsequent ascents and descents

By 2015, a total of over 7000 summittings had been recorded, achieved by over 4000 unique climbers of whom 9% were female. Most of the climbers who have summitted multiple times are Sherpas. Ascent from the south (Nepal) remains more popular than from the north (Tibet). The death rate on both routes is similar (4%), but the number of deaths varies greatly from one year to the next. Of all deaths, 36% befall the tiny minority (3%) of climbers who try to summit without supplemental oxygen.

Nearly all Nepal expeditions use the Hillary-Tenzing route through the Khumbu Icefall, Western Cwm and South Col. For a realistic account of what the climb is like, read Harry Kikstra's book: see page 78.

The death rate has dropped since the 1990s – due to the greater professionalism of commercial operations, better equipment and more accurate weather forecasting. However, tragedy still strikes. In a single day in 1996, for example, eight climbers died in a freak storm. In April 2014, an avalanche in the Khumbu Icefall killed 16 Sherpas. A year later, the earthquake triggered an avalanche that killed more than 19 people. Avalanches are the leading cause of death among Sherpas: their work obliges them to spend long days in avalanche-prone areas, ferrying loads and setting up ropes, ladders and camps for clients. Of the 282 people who died on Everest up to August 2015, 60% were westerners and 40% Sherpas.

There is a short weather window when approaching monsoons temporarily shift the jet stream upward. The number of climbers competing for access in causes dangerous congestion. Historically, about 70% of all summits are achieved between 13-22 May.

The price of an Everest climb lies in the range $30,000-$85,000, depending on the level of support and the nationality of your guide: western guides can add $10,000-$25,000 to the price. Prices tend to be about $10,000 lower from the Tibetan side, partly because permits are cheaper and also because its Base Camp can be reached by vehicle, whereas the Nepal climb begins with a week-long trek. The cost in human life and limb must also be reckoned.

Page 36: Everest's summit towers over its West Ridge (far left)

Page 37: Nuptse (7864 m), screening Lhotse behind

Everest records

- **First ascent without supplemental oxygen:** Reinhold Messner and Peter Habeler, 1978
- **Fastest ascent from Everest Base Camp (Nepal) using oxygen (8 hours 10 minutes):** Pemba Dorje, 2004
- **Most frequent summiteers (21 times):** Apa Sherpa and Phurba Tashi Sherpa in 2011 and 2013 respectively
- **Oldest person to climb Mount Everest (aged 80 years):** Yuichiro Miura in 2013
- **Youngest person to summit successfully (aged 13 years):** Jordan Romero, USA, in 2010
- **First summit to Base Camp ski descent without removing skis (4 hours 40 minutes):** Davo Karničar, 2000

Trekking hours 4-7
Altitude at start 2840 m 9320 ft
Altitude gain overall nil: descend 350 m/1150ft, then re-ascend
Summary An exciting first day that includes the Lukla landing, swaying suspension bridges over mighty rivers, lush vegetation and fine views – a classic introduction to Himalayan trekking.

- You leave Kathmandu for the airport very early in the morning, hoping to find that your flight to Lukla will depart on schedule, or at least on the scheduled day. Weather conditions are less favourable for flying in the heat of the day, and Lukla airport closes when visibility is poor or winds too strong.

- The 45-minute flight is an adventure in itself, with wonderful views over the green foothills of the Himalaya from a small turbo-prop plane. Nervous flyers may wish to consider the alternative, which is an all-day bus journey from Kathmandu to Jiri, followed by a 6-9-day trek to Lukla. To view videos of Lukla landings and take-offs, visit our page *www.rucsacs.com/links/tte.*

- Lukla airport was renamed the Hillary-Tenzing airport in 2008 and has one of the world's most extreme approaches. Pilots have to cope with thin air at altitude, fast-changing mountain weather with crosswinds and aim for a runway that's only 527 m long (1730 ft) and ends in a high stone wall. To stop in time, the pilot needs full reverse thrust and hard braking, assisted by the upward slope (gradient of 12%). A round of applause after a safe landing is the norm. (Taking off downhill is also quite exciting, but most people are more relaxed when homeward-bound.)

- If you are lucky enough to arrive in Lukla in the early morning , you may take breakfast before trekking down towards Phakding. The broad trail heads northward away from the airport passing through a *kani* (entrance gateway) with prayer wheels.

- Descending past farmland, you reach the settlement of Choplung. Soon you'll catch your first glimpse of the mighty Dudh Kosi river, your companion all the way to Phunki Tenga (beyond Namche).

Plane taking off on Lukla's downhill runway

- After some minor undulations, the trail passes through Thadokoshi, dropping sharply to cross its river, the Thadokoshi Khola, by suspension bridge. In clear conditions, there are fine views eastward up its gorge towards Kusum Kanguru (6367 m), a difficult 'trekking peak'.

Mani wall below Monjo

- After the bridge, you climb a flight of steps, round a corner and in under 1 km descend to the scattered village of Ghat (2490 m). You have now lost 350 m of altitude since leaving Lukla, but don't worry: from here on, the long climb begins.

- It'a about another 2 km to the beginning of Phakding, preceded by the luxury lodge buildings of Farakpa Village Resort. Phakding is at 2610m/8560ft, so you'll have re-gained 120 m of altitude once you reach it. The village is in two parts, separated by nearly 1 km including a long suspension bridge over the river. Some groups stop for the night here, whilst others continue to Monjo (2840 m/9320 ft).

- If overnighting in Phakding, go for an acclimatisation walk in the afternoon. One option is to cross the suspension bridge as if continuing to Monjo, but turn off left, steeply uphill through the forest, to visit the fine Penacholing monastery there. It enjoys a wonderful situation about 200 m above the village, and is over 350 years old.

Penacholing monastery, interior

To continue to Monjo, you cross the Dudh Kosi river, and turn right to follow it upstream. Within 1 km you cross a tributary, then pass through Toktok. *En route* for Bengkar, you pass a tall, slender waterfall.

About 600 m after Bengkar you re-cross the Dudh Kosi by a Swiss-built suspension bridge and continue up the east bank to Chumoa. Here you cross another tributary, the Monjo Khola, before reaching Monjo. That will take about 2-3 hours from Phakding.

Waterfall near Bengkar

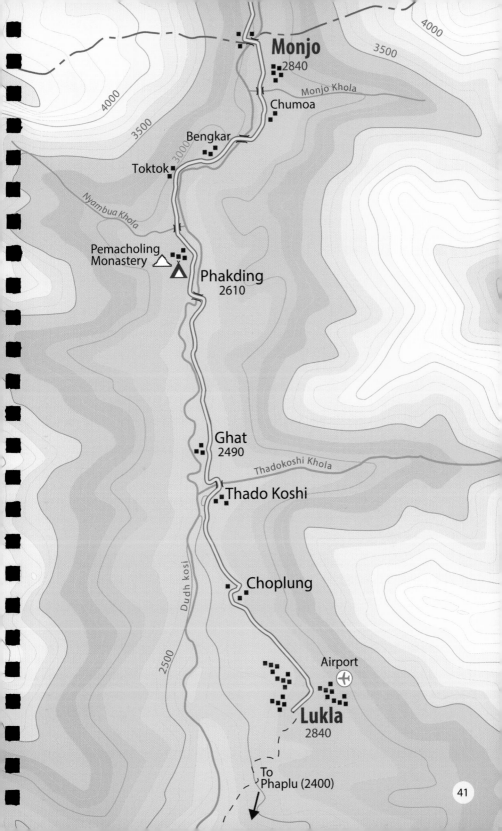

Monjo
2840

Monjo Khola

Chumoa

Bengkar

Toktok

Nyambua Khola

Pemacholing
Monastery

Phakding
2610

Ghat
2490

Thadokoshi Khola

Thado Koshi

Dudh kosi

Choplung

Airport

Lukla
2840

To
Phaplu (2400)

4000

3500

3500

3000

2500

3·2 Monjo to Namche Bazaar

Trekking hours 3-5
Altitude at start 2840 m 9320 ft
Altitude gain 600 m 1970 ft
Summary The first day of serious altitude gain, rising through forested hillside and ending with a long, punishing hill up to Namche; if the weather is clear, you will be rewarded with a distant view of Everest's summit.

- Just after Monjo, everybody stops at the Sagarmāthā National Park Centre to buy entry permits. There are toilets behind the main building. Stepping through the kani into the National Park, you may see a fine view of the mountain north of Namche, the Khumbila (5761 m).

Khumbila, from near Monjo

- Descend to cross the Dudh Kosi by another long, wobbly suspension bridge, soon reaching the lodges of Jorsale (2805 m/9200 ft) on its west bank. This is the last accommodation before Namche, which lies over 600 m vertically above you.

- The trail climbs out of Jorsale, but dips to re-cross the river twice more. Your final crossing before Namche is the high suspension bridge at the confluence of the Dudh and Bhote Kosi rivers.

- You now embark on Namche Hill – a steep climb with 600 m/1970 ft of altitude gain, tough but achievable as long as you pace yourself sensibly. The trail climbs by a series of zigzags through pine forest that provides some welcome shade. Over halfway up, at a bend, there is an obvious rest stop which offers, on a clear day, your first view of Everest and Lhotse: step a few metres to the right to see this.

- About half an hour later, you enter the outskirts of Namche Bazaar, the *de facto* Sherpa capital of the region. From the moment that you first glimpse Namche's buildings, be prepared for a further long climb: the village is extensive, its 'streets' mostly steep alleys or stone staircases, and your lodge will probably be near the top of the village.

Confluence of the Dudh and Bhote Kosi rivers

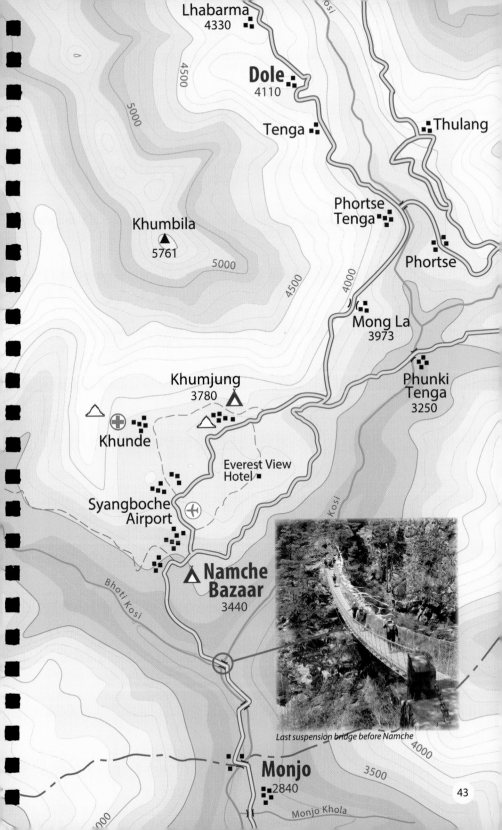

Lhabarma
4330

Dole
4110

Tenga

Thulang

Phortse
Tenga

Phortse

Khumbila
5761

Mong La
3973

Khumjung
3780

Phunki
Tenga
3250

Khunde

Everest View
Hotel

Syangboche
Airport

Namche
Bazaar
3440

Bhoti Kosi

Kosi

Last suspension bridge before Namche

Monjo
2840

Monjo Khola

Namche is a thriving centre filled with lodges, internet cafés, money changers, restaurants and cafés and shops selling cheap gear and souvenirs. It's the trading heart of the Khumbu Valley. Saturdays are special, when it hosts the regional market or bazaar. To see this in full swing, you need to be up and around in the morning: by noon, most traders are packing up.

Saturday market, Namche Bazaar

Namche's situation is striking: built on a natural amphitheatre, its multi-coloured buildings pepper the hillside. Its backdrop is the thrilling ridge of Kwangde (6187 m).

Most groups stay here for at least two nights. Even if you only make a walking tour of Namche, you will gain some benefit from its steep alleys. However, most people do an acclimatisation walk on their rest day. Head up the hill north-east of the village for a great view of the valley, including Ama Dablam and Everest. Or visit the twin villages of Khumjung and Khunde, gaining up to 400 m of altitude. Hillary built his first school in Khumjung, and first hospital in Khunde. There is also a monastery with an alleged Yeti scalp – which is, however, a fake.

Stupa in upper Namche, with Kwangde as backdrop

3·3 Namche Bazaar to Tengboche

Trekking hours **4-6**
Altitude at start **3440 m 11,290 ft**
Altitude gain **420 m 1970 ft**
Summary **Above Namche, there are still plenty of trees, and mountain views are at first dominated by the elegant Ama Dablam; the day ends at the atmospheric Tengboche monastery.**

- Climb out of Namche from its eastern edge, past the National Park headquarters and army post. The main trail contours the hillside some 600 m/2000 ft above the river.

- Within half an hour, you round a bend to the finest panorama so far: the valley is dominated by the slender outline of Ama Dablam (6856 m) to the right, with Everest, Nuptse and Lhotse in the distance and the foaming rapids of the Dudh Kosi far below.

- Shortly afterwards, you come to prayer flags and a white chorten built in 2003 to commemorate the 50th anniversary of Tenzing Norgay's climb to Everest's summit and the Sherpas who made it possible.

- After a further half hour or so, ignore a junction (for Khumjung and Gokyo), keeping right along the main trail. You'll continue to enjoy excellent views of the great peaks of the Khumbu – Everest, Lhotse, Nuptse and Ama Dablam. You may be able to spot Tengboche's monastery, far ahead to the right, perched on a forested ridge.

- After passing several settlements and mani walls, the track descends by zigzags and stone steps to the river. Cross to its east bank at Phunki Tenga (3250 m), where water power turns the prayer wheels. This is your last crossing of the Dudh Kosi, which drains the Gokyo valley. From here you'll follow the Imja Khola upstream.

Chorten, with Ama Dablam beyond

- It's probably taken two to three hours since Namche, with a loss of 200 m of altitude. The climb to reach Tengboche, over 600 m above Phunki, will take about as long again.

- This climb is very comparable to Namche Hill, and seems tough because of altitude, and much of it passes through lush forest where progress is hard to assess. However, there are some open stretches where you'll see fine views back to Kwangde's snowy ridge, and also Thamserku to your right. Keep an eye out for Danphe pheasants and wild goats (Thar) in this section.

- Near the top of Tengboche's spectacular ridge, you pass through a kani with fine mandalas, and very soon after you reach the chorten announcing the largest Buddhist monastery in Nepal. Established in this remote location in 1916, it has since been destroyed and rebuilt twice. Almost inaccessible until the first half of last century, it now receives thousands of visitors each year. Minor damage from the 2015 earthquake was soon repaired.

- If you stay at a lodge in Tengboche, aim to visit the early morning service before setting off. The monks chanting, their musical instruments and their tea ritual create an unforgettable experience. (There's also an afternoon service, but it tends to be busier with tourists and its timing is harder to reconcile with trekking schedules.)

- Visitors are allowed inside, and even to take photographs (no flash): see the photo on page 34. Donations are welcome, and you can visit also the EcoCentre. Some groups take an acclimatisation day here: it's both higher and quieter than Namche.

- Staying in Tengboche also lets you enjoy its early morning all-round mountain views: to the north are Cholatse and Taboche. North-east, you'll see the Nupstse ridge (but not its summit), Everest, Lhotse and Lhotse Shar. Ama Dablam dominates the view to the east, and to the south-east lie Thamserku and Kangtega.

Gateway to Tengboche monastery

Thare

Dudh Kosi

Thulang

Pangboche

3930

Phortse
Tenga

Phortse

4000

Mong La
3973

Imja Khola

Monastery

Deboche

△Tengboche
3860

Phunki
Tenga
3250

Dudh Kosi

5000

4500

Bridge over the Dudh Khosi

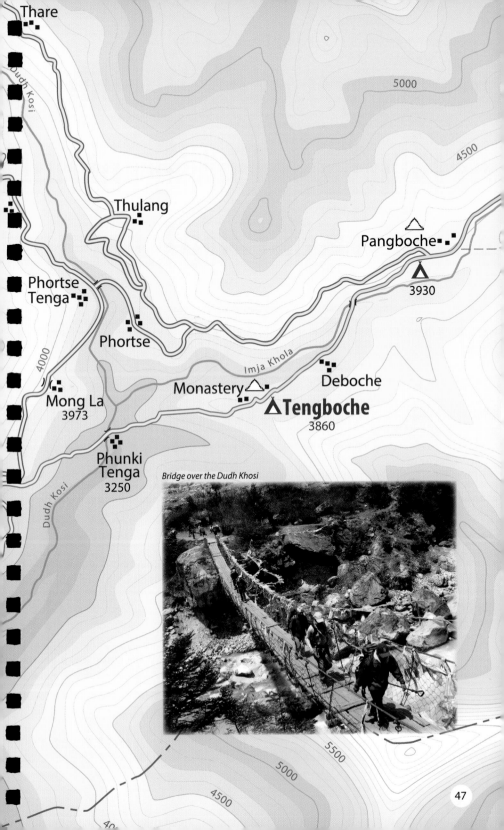

5500

5000

4500

40

Trekking hours	4-6
Altitude at start	3860 m 12,660 ft
Altitude gain	415 m (to Pheriche) or 550 m (to Dingboche)
Summary	This is the last section to feature forest, and it involves a marked altitude gain to Pheriche, with an even greater one to Dingboche.

- Continue through the forest, enjoying the sight and smell of lush vegetation – juniper, berberis, pine, birch, rhododendron and Himalayan fir. Once you've climbed above the tree line later today, you'll miss them.

- The trail descends through Deboche (3820 m/12,520 ft) – an alternative overnight stop if Tengboche is booked out. Fine views of Ama Dablam still dominate to the east.

Crossing the Lobuche Khola

- After descending a bit more, you cross the Imja Khola at its narrows to the north bank. From here you climb slightly to reach Pangboche (3930 m/12,890ft) within 2 hours (or less) of setting out.

Pangboche, with Ama Dablam

- Pangboche is in two parts, and makes a good place for a break or even to overnight for further acclimatisation. Its lower village is the larger, but it's the upper village that is home to the oldest monastery in the Khumbu valley. This is well worth a visit for its amazing wood carvings and historic atmosphere.

- After leaving Pangboche, cross two small tributaries of the Imja Khola, separated by about 2 km of easy, level trail. Continue for another 1.5 km until you reach the handful of buildings that comprise Tsuro Og (4135 m/13,565 ft).

- The route divides here, left for Pheriche or right to Dingboche. The choice will already have been made, and is not important. Whichever one you stay in, the other is only a short hike away. Pheriche is apt to be colder, because more wind-swept than

Carving, Pangboche monastery

Dingboche, which also has very fine views of Lhotse. But Pheriche has the Himalayan Research Association clinic which may offer a daily lecture. It also has a steel sculpture inscribed with the names of all who have died on Everest: see page 50.

Approaching Pheriche

- If you keep left to stay in the valley of the Lobuche Khola river, crossing it only after a further 1 km, you'll arrive in Pheriche (4275 m/14,030 ft) about 2-3 hours after leaving Pangboche.

- Alternatively, bear right to cross the river straight away and head uphill (now on the left bank of the Imja Khola) to Dingboche (4410 m/14,470 ft), a larger village in a side valley leading towards Island Peak and Lhotse.

- Whichever village is chosen, most groups spend two nights there, and go for an acclimatisation walk on the spare day. Some climb towards Nankgar Tsang and top out at over 5000 m near its peak, or make a much longer trek up the valley of the Imja Khola towards Chukhung Ri (5500 m/18210 ft). Others settle for the pleasant round trip over the ridge between Pheriche and DIngboche, with some stiff gradients but the added interest of seeing the other village, and perhaps sampling its food.

Sculpture naming deaths on Everest, Pheriche

Dingboche, early morning

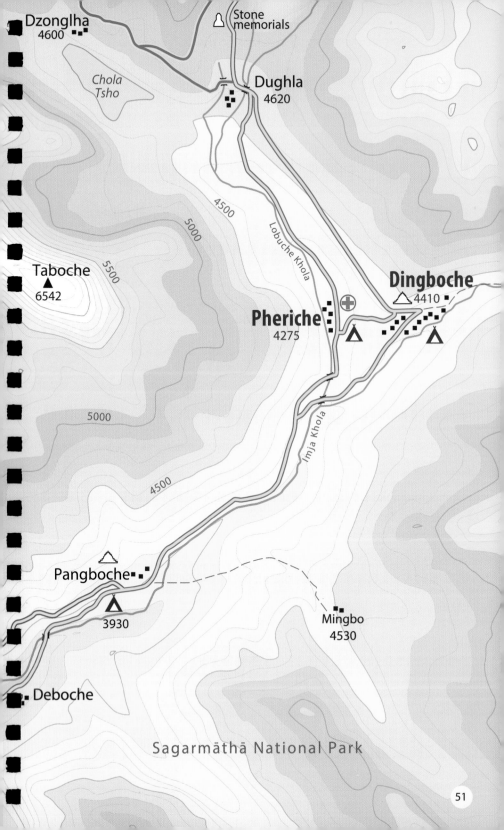

Dzonglha
4600

Stone
memorials

Dughla
4620

Chola
Tsho

4500

5000

Lobuche Khola

Taboche
6542

5500

Pheriche
4275

Dingboche
4410

5000

Imja Khola

4500

Pangboche
3930

Mingbo
4530

Deboche

Sagarmāthā National Park

51

3·5 Pheriche or Dingboche to Lobuche

Trekking hours 4-5

Altitude at start 4275 m (Pheriche) or 4410 m (Dingboche)

Altitude gain 635 m (from Pheriche) or 500 m (from Dingboche)

Summary Another day with a considerable gain in altitude, especially from Pheriche; above Dughla, you pass stone memorials and trek beside the Khumbu Glacier.

Up the valley from Pheriche, towards the moraine

- Leave Pheriche to hike north-westward up the flat-bottomed valley – a rocky trail with some grassy bits – for under 2 km, bearing right where it branches off uphill. You cross a number of streams on the way, but there are plenty of stepping-stones.

- Soon you start to climb in earnest, up the Khumbu Glacier's terminal moraine, the route veering round to the right as it climbs more steeply. There are fine views of Taboche and Cholatse across to your left (west).

- Continue climbing uphill among the rocks until you cross a small bridge over a glacial stream. This leads to Dughla, a good spot to rest and refresh after some hiking, or even to overnight for further acclimatisation.

- The walk from Dingboche to Dughla takes a similar length of time. You head west at first, climbing the sandy track up the short steep hill and heading down the other side. From here on, you are walking parallel to the Pheriche route, but 150 m or so higher, and with even better views of Taboche and Cholatse beyond the valley to the west.

Terminal moraine, Khumbu Glacier

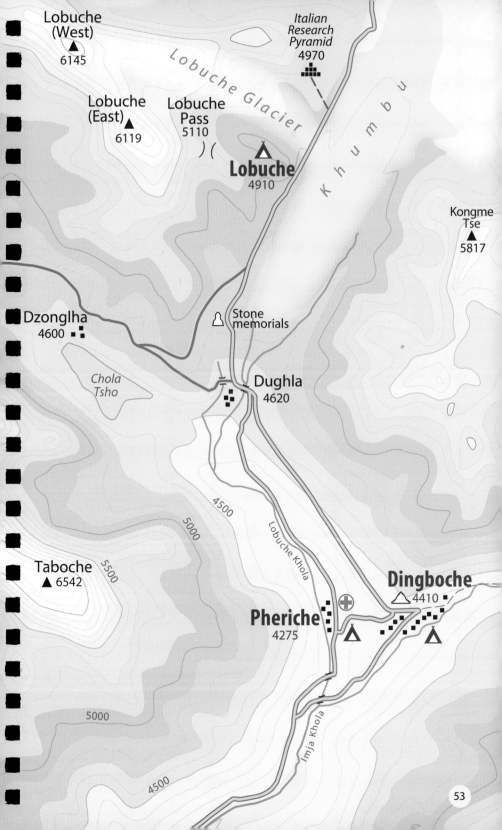

Lobuche
(West)
▲
6145

Lobuche
(East) ▲
6119

Lobuche
Pass
5110

) (

Lobuche Glacier

*Italian
Research
Pyramid*
4970

⛰ **Lobuche**
4910

K h u m b u

Kongme
Tse
▲
5817

Dzonglha
4600 ▪▪

*Chola
Tsho*

⛰ Stone
memorials

Dughla
4620

4500

Lobuche Khola

5000

Taboche
▲ 6542

5500

Dingboche
△ 4410

Pheriche
4275

⛺

⛺

5000

Imja Khola

4500

- After Dughla (4620 m/15,160 ft), you climb the moraine for an hour or more on a tough rocky path, gaining 200 m to reach a small pass and plateau with many cairns, chortens and prayer flags. The cairns are memorials for those who died on Everest, mainly Sherpas. It's a sombre reminder of their hard work and the dangers they face in their efforts to help clients to realise their dreams.

Memorial cairn to Scott Fischer (1955-1996)

- Shortly after the memorials, notice a track leading sharp back left (south-west) and uphill. This leads to the classic trek to Gokyo passing over the Cho La via Dzonghla: see pages 71-75.

- For now, keep climbing the trail on the left of the Khumbu Glacier's moraine until you reach the collection of lodges at Lobuche – a cold, windy place with modest facilities.

- If you arrive early enough, you could visit the 'Pyramid' (the Italian Research Centre for weather and seismic data) after lunch: continue up the trail toward Gorak Shep and turn left after 1 km. Or scramble up to the glacier or the hills around the village before settling down in front of the yak-dung stoves with a bowl of soup or plenty of tea, to rest and acclimatise further.

Morning view from Lobuche

3·6 Lobuche to Gorak Shep

Trekking hours 2-4
Altitude at start 4910 m 16,110 ft
Altitude gain 230 m 750 ft
Summary Although the altitude gain is not great, this section is surprisingly tiring, because of rough terrain and high altitude; warm sleeping gear is essential for overnighting at Gorak Shep.

Italian Research Centre above Lobuche

- Continue along the west side of the Khumbu Glacier, within 1 km passing (or following) the left turn to the Italian Research Centre (Pyramid) which collects weather and seismic data.

- The glacier mostly looks grey, not white as you might expect, being covered in rocks, scree and debris. The trail undulates, and becomes rough in places where you cross various side moraines.

- After rounding a bend, if skies are clear, the elegant snow-clad cone of Pumori comes into view ahead, with Kala Pattar looking deceptively tame in front.

- Climb any of the tracks up towards Lobuche Pass (5110 m/16,770 ft) and cross the confluence of two glaciers (Changri Nup and Changri Shar) which together join the Khumbu Glacier here.

Lingtren (6713 m) from near Gorak Shep

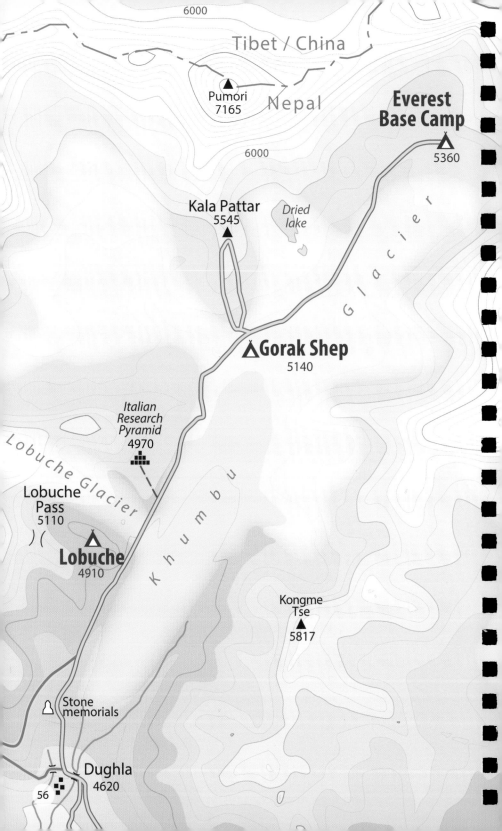

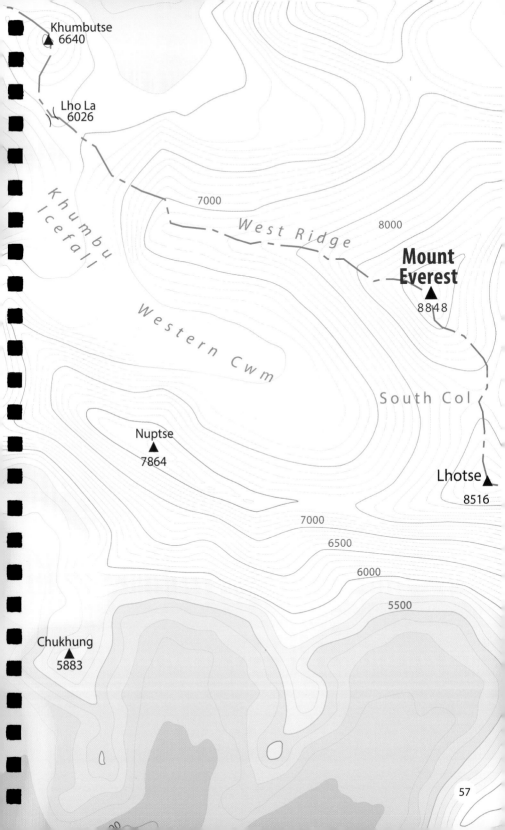

Khumbutse
6640

Lho La
6026

Khumbu
Icefall

7000

West Ridge

8000

**Mount
Everest**
8848

Western Cwm

South Col

Nuptse
7864

Lhotse
8516

7000

6500

6000

5500

Chukhung
5883

Soon after, you round a bend and see the guesthouses of Gorak Shep some distance below. Like Lobuche, it exists only to service the needs of trekkers and climbers, but at 5140 m/16,860 ft, Gorak Shep is the highest settlement in the world. It sits above a dry lake-bed, and there is another lake (usually frozen) to its north. Gorak Shep is known for very cold nights and great mountain views.

Most people who want to climb Kala Pattar and/or visit Base Camp stay in Gorak Shep for one or two nights. (Remember that staying at EBC involves camping in tents, so it has to be planned ahead.) There are various options for combining excursions, but in general we would advise trekkers to climb Kala Pattar first, then spend another night at Gorak Shep. Next day, if still feeling fine, continue to Base Camp: see page 62.

Dried lake, Gorak Shep

Kala Pattar could be climbed the same day that you arrive in Gorak Shep – if you're well acclimatised and have the energy. However, its views are often obscured by cloud in the afternoon and it may be better to postpone it to the next morning anyway. It can also be climbed after a day spent visiting EBC and returning to Gorak Shep.

It's also possible to climb Kala Pattar without staying at Gorak Shep first, by setting off very early from Lobuche, say about 3 or 4 am. After trekking in the dark for a few hours, have breakfast in Gorak Shep and set off again about 7 or 8 am for a morning climb before overnighting at Gorak Shep. This makes for a long hard day, but those who suffer from altitude and coldness at night may prefer to sleep at Lobuche. Be prepared for changes of plan depending on local weather conditions and the health and fitness of the group.

Gorak Shep

3·7 Ascent of Kala Pattar

Kala Pattar (5545 m/18,190 ft) is not a separate mountain, but a prominent peak on the south ridge of the mountain Pumori (7165 m/23,505 ft). Don't be deceived by the modest aspect that it presents from Gorak Shep. It's a steep, tiring ascent at high altitude, and its summit section involves some boulder-hopping and scrambling. Take plenty of water, and ensure it does not freeze, and take also warm clothing so you can linger long enough to enjoy the legendary summit views

From Gorak Shep, the climb involves an altitude gain of 405 m/1330 ft, and takes about 3-4 hours for the round trip, plus time on the summit.

Starting the ascent, Pumori ahead

Start by crossing the dry lake and go up the other side on sandy switchbacks. There are two obvious routes: the left one goes directly up the spur, and may be preferable after recent snowfall, but the slightly less steep one to the right is generally used.

It begins as a sandy path with steep switchbacks that demand a slow pace. After a while, the gradient eases and there's a wonderful middle section which traverses the hillside with ever-finer views opening up.

Then the route becomes steeper again, with a sting in its tail. The final scramble to the cairn with prayer flags demands a fresh surge of energy. The summit area is tiny, so depending on how many others are competing for space, you can move to the small plateau just below, where movement is easier and the view just as good.

And what a view! This mountain panorama may be the highlight of your entire trip, encompassing (from north to east) Pumori, Changtse, Khumbutse and mighty Everest itself, with the West Ridge standing proud to the left of its summit, looking like another peak. You can identify the Khumbu Icefall, Base Camp and the South Col. This is the closest view of Everest accessible to trekkers, as opposed to mountaineers.

Everest
Base Camp

The unexpected star of the show is Nuptse, to the east, which appears taller than Everest despite being 970 m lower: see pages 36-7. This illusion is caused by Everest's summit being nearly twice as far away as Nuptse's. Nupste looks stunningly beautiful, with its fluted shoulders and shapely peak: see our title page photo, taken from here.

Left to right: Changtse, Everest West Ridge and summit, shoulder of Nuptse

Summit cairn, Kala Pattar

3·8 Gorak Shep to Everest Base Camp

Trekking hours	**2-4 (each way)**
Altitude at start	**5140 m 16,860 ft**
Altitude gain	**220 m 720 ft**
Summary	**Strenuous in each direction, the altitude gain is only part of the challenge; very rough terrain makes the journey tougher, and the trek culminates at EBC.**

The last section to Base Camp takes 2-4 hours on the way up, and almost as long again on the return 'downhill' because of the very rough, undulating terrain. If you are visiting EBC as a day trip, not camping there, leave Gorak Shep early to avoid running out of daylight.

The track continues beyond the lake at Gorak Shep and meanders beside the glacier on the crest of its lateral moraine. After 1 km or so, the route heads across the glacier itself, veering right (north-east).

Base Camp is a large collection of tents on a slow-moving river of ice, so its exact location varies from year to year. Most expeditions choose to camp at about 5360 m, near the snout of the Khumbu Icefall.

Trekker en route for Base Camp

The Icefall is a notoriously dangerous section of the Everest ascent route, a tortuous jumble of crevasses and seracs – unstable blocks of ice as tall as office buildings. Although the lower end is less dangerous than the notorious higher parts that have claimed so many lives, take advice and check local conditions before exploring it.

The terrain of the Base Camp area is surprisingly hard going, and out of season, it will be completely deserted. If you have seen it clearly from Kala Pattar, you may see little point in going there. Over the years, many good camping spots have been developed, and during the main summit climbing seasons, the whole area is like a temporary village. It will be covered in multicoloured tents of all shapes and sizes, with a huge range of facilities, including bakeries and expedition communications centres.

Khumbu Glacier, detail

Everest Base Camp

3·9 Everest Base Camp to Lukla

Trekking hours **14-21 spread over three days**

Altitude at start **5360 m 17,590 ft**

Altitude loss **2520 m 8270 ft**

Summary **Some trekkers find the descent the most relaxing part of the trip; for others, it leads to the strenuous trek to Gokyo and a new beginning.**

It is easy to forget about the descent. Depending on your route option, it may still be a major part of the trek. Even if you need to descend quickly and by the same route as you ascended, the EBC trek is a very different experience in the reverse direction. With the pressure off, goals achieved, altitude issues receding or resolved, it can be a delightful experience.

Although descending is physically easier than climbing, it can be hard on the knees, especially protracted descents like Namche to Jorsale, and poles may be very useful, especially for mature trekkers. Also, it isn't all downhill: you may be surprised at how much the trail undulates, especially from EBC back to Gorak Shep. Groups vary in the pace they set for the descent, but it generally takes two days to reach Namche and one further day to reach Lukla.

On the descent, you will enjoy different perspectives, see the mountains from new angles and take fresh photos. In a more relaxed mood, you may engage more with your Sherpa team and local people. You may stop at different villages or teahouses e.g. if you ascended via Pheriche you will perhaps descend via Dingboche – or *vice versa*.

Most groups descend from Namche to Lukla in a single day, perhaps with a lunch stop at Phakding. Keep some energy in reserve for the final (350 m vertical) climb to Lukla, and get an early night before the next morning's very early start for a plane back to Kathmandu. Some groups split Lukla-Namche over two days, but this may depend on the organiser's confidence about the Lukla departure, and whether there are spare days in Kathmandu before the international flights home. Be prepared for a possible extra night in Lukla if the weather dictates.

If your itinerary includes the ambitious trek to Gokyo over the Cho La (see pages 71-75), you will depart from the standard EBC route just south of Lobuche. You then, after an easy day to Dzonghla, face the strenuous ascent to the Cho La (5368 m) and may choose to climb Gokyo Ri (5357 m) a day or so afterwards. In physical terms, then, your true descent will begin only after you leave Gokyo.

Morning after a cold night at EBC

Trekking hours	5-7
Altitude at start	3440 m 11,290 ft
Altitude gain	670 m 2200 ft
Summary	This section describes two days-worth of trekking with serious altitude gain; some groups divide it at Khumjung, others at Phortse Tenga.

The Gokyo valley offers many advantages over the standard EBC route. It used to be called 'Death Valley' by rescue pilots, but only because the shorter distances tempted impatient trekkers to ascend too fast to acclimatise. Gokyo, although 120 m lower than Lobuche, is still a high-altitude village at 4790 m/15,720 ft, so take your time.

- Begin from Lukla with the trek to Namche described on pages 38-44. From Namche, many groups take the trail to Khumjung and overnight there, at 3780 m. It's only a 2-3 hour hike, but there's plenty to see, including a monastery and the first school that Ed Hillary built for Sherpa children.

- Next morning, a detour to the Everest View hotel offers a spectacular mountain panorama, with Everest at centre stage. After returning to Khumjung, you descend and there's then a choice of trails towards Dole. (One stays higher for longer, the other descends to meet the EBC route sooner.) Either way, from Khumjung to Dole will take about 5-6 hours: see below.

- Alternatively, leave Namche to the north-east on the EBC trail that hugs the hillside high above the river, hovering around the 3600 m contour. Leave this route to join the trail from Khumjung at a well-marked junction about 4 km beyond Namche: see page 45, bullet 4.

- The long, steady climb to Mong is helped by flights of stone steps. Mong is the birthplace of Lama Sange Dorje who is said to have brought Buddhism to the Khumbu valley. Enjoy fine views over the mountains and the Dudh Kosi, with the village of Phortse perhaps visible on the far side of the river.

*Over Khumjung: Ama Dablam (distant left),
Kangtega and Thamserku at right*

- Attaining the Mong La (the pass) at 3973 m/13,030 ft is a major milestone. It features prayer flags and guards the entrance to the Gokyo valley, with stunning views if the weather is clear. The crest makes a great lunch stop, and small groups may even overnight here if there is room in the lodge.

- From here, the trail descends in sharp zigzags, steeper than the ascent, almost to the river. The village of Phortse Tenga (3680 m/12,070 ft) makes a delightful overnight stop – albeit not quite as good for acclimatisation as Khumjung which is 100 m higher.

- Just beyond the village of Phortse Tenga, there's a junction where a right turn across the Dudh Kosi would take you to Phortse. However, the Gokyo trail continues on the west side of the river, north-west towards Dole.

Waterfall below Dole

- Climbing through forests of rhododendron, pine and fir, you pass a National Park checkpoint and army outpost. On a clear day, look north for your first glimpse of Cho Oyu (8201 m). Twisting up steeply through woodland, the trail climbs stone steps, crosses several streams and passes below waterfalls.

- The trail climbs the hillside, diverging further from the river, crossing a ridge and ascending to the grazing around Dole (4110 m). Keep an eye on the view behind you: in clear weather there are fine views all the way to Kangtega and Thamserku.

The Mong La

4·2 Dole to Machhermo

Trekking hours 2-3

Altitude at start 4110 m 13,480 ft

Altitude gain 3600 m 1180 ft

Summary **This is a short, easy day with increasingly fine mountain views, and a significant altitude gain – a section to relish at leisure.**

- This is a short day, with a moderate distance but still 360 m of altitude gain. Tree cover becomes sparse, but the mountain and river views are very fine. As you head north, the snowy massif of Cho Oyu, sixth highest mountain in the world, becomes increasingly prominent at the head of the valley. You may also identify the shapely Gyachung Kang (7952 m) to its right, distant on the Tibetan border.

- The trail descends to cross the Phule Khola river, then traverses yak grazing hillside, with some mani stones and teahouses. Up to Lhabarma (4330 m) is a stiff climb, and it's a relief to reach the long section above the river that follows the contours.

- Less than two hours after Dole, the trail dips slightly to the small hamlet of Luza (4390 m/14,400 ft), sitting in a slight basin. Originally a yak grazing area, this now also has some lodges for trekkers.

- Climb out of Luza, passing a chorten with prayer flags, and enjoy great views of Cholatse and Taboche to your right. After half an hour of undulating trail, you reach the lovely sheltered village of Machhermo (4470 m/14,665 ft) which has a medical post.

- It is also home to a widely-believed yeti legend: in1974, a young Sherpani met a yeti in Machhermo which knocked her down and killed three of her yaks. She ran home and reported it in Khunde. A police team went to investigate, and found huge, unexplained footprints.

South over Dole, with Phortse across the valley

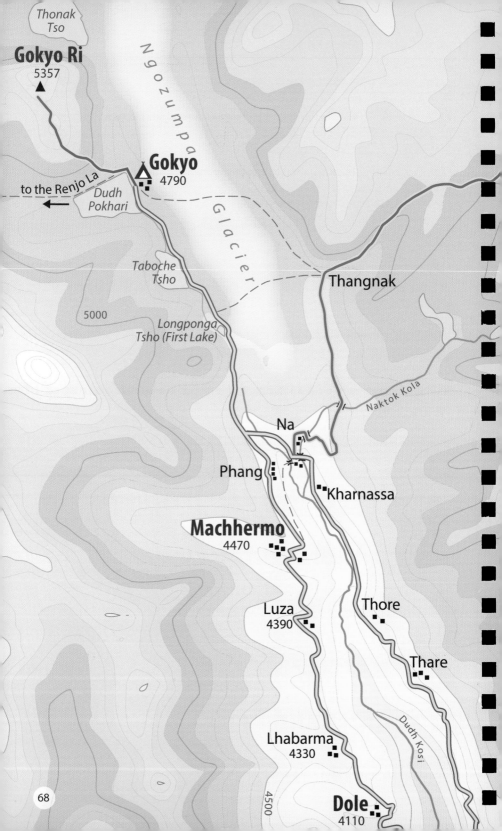

Gokyo Ri
5357
▲

Thonak
Tso

Ngozumpa

Gokyo
4790

to the Renjo La ←

Dudh
Pokhari

Glacier

Taboche
Tsho

Thangnak

5000

Longponga
Tsho (First Lake)

Naktok Kola

Na

Phang

Kharnassa

Machhermo
4470

Thore

Luza
4390

Thare

Dudh Kosi

Lhabarma
4330

4500

Dole
4110

Trekking hours 3-4
Altitude at start 4470 m 14,2967ft
Altitude gain 320 m 1050 ft
Summary As you ascend the valley, the mountain views become more impressive and glacial features – moraines, lakes and the huge glacier itself – become more dominant.

Machhermo

- Descend fairly steeply to cross the Machhermo Khola river, beyond which lies most of the village (including its rescue post). The Gokyo trail bears left to climb steeply northward; another trail heads east, then north, to cross two rivers at Na before looping south, eventually reaching Phortse.

- From a high point of about 4450 m/14,600 ft marked by prayer flags, the trail descends slightly to the farm buildings at Phang, near the tragic site of an avalanche that in 1995 killed over 40 people.

Rocky staircase

- From Phang, you climb about 160 m/525 ft over the next 2 km to reach the First Lake, passing the terminal moraine of the Ngozumpa Glacier. This steepish ascent follows any of the braided paths up a juniper-clad hillside.

- Further up, the sandy path is punctuated by rocky staircases and is hemmed in by sheer cliffs to your left and huge boulders on the right. The First Lake is small and unimpressive, but it is spring fed and never freezes over completely.

- At the end of the lake, opposite rapids to your left, a trail across the Ngozumpa Glacier veers off to the right. The Gokyo trail continues northerly, running alongside the glacier.

- Within 500 m of the glacier trail junction, you reach the Second Lake (Taboche Tsho or Longponga), much more impressive than the first. There's a rest spot here, with stone bench seating and a splendid view of the lake, with fine mountains as its backdrop, and the even more imposing view north to Cho Oyu.

- As you climb the valley, the mountains to your right become ever more prominent: Lobuche Peak, Cholatse, Taboche and Kangtega. About 600 m beyond the end of the Second Lake, you reach the Third Lake or Dudh Pokhari, its turquoise waters framed by snow-fringed mountains. After rounding a few corners in the path, you reach a stone cairn with prayer flags, heralding your arrival at Gokyo itself (4790 m/15720 ft).

Gokyo also has a path leading west to Renjo La, one of the passes on the Three Passes Trail: see map listing on page 79. Another trail heads north up the valley to the upper lakes. The fourth lake (Thonak Tsho, 4870 m) is only about 3 km north, and has high cliffs and is framed by impressive peaks. A further 4 km brings you to the fifth lake (Ngozumba Tsho, 4990 m) and the trail continues to Scoundrel's Viewpoint, with legendary mountain views. The sixth lake lies just beyond, still further north.

The village also faces Gokyo Ri (5357 m), the peak that for many trekkers is the prime focus of the visit: see page 76. Spending several nights in Gokyo is ideal, because it means you can choose to climb Gokyo Ri when the visibility is good, and make lower-level hikes at other times.

Descending direct to Namche, a distance of about 20 km, can be done in a single long day, with possible meal stops at Machhermo and Phortse Tenga. If there is no rush, taking two days will be more relaxing, and some groups descend down the east side of the valley, leaving the ascent route at Machhermo towards Na. Namche to Lukla is also a longish day, but an easier distance and at lower altitudes.

For some, there's also the adventurous option to make Gokyo the start of an itinerary that crosses the Cho La into the Khumbu Valley and then continues to Everest Base Camp. See page 6 for an overview of the options, and pages 71-5 for a description of the link made westward from Lobuche.

Gokyo, with Cho Oyu distant

4·4 Lobuche to Gokyo by the Cho La

Day 1 Lobuche to Dzonghla 2-3 hours
Day 2 Dzonghla to Thangnak via the Cho La 5-8 hours
Day 3 Thangnak to Gokyo 2-4 hours

This section describes an adventurous route that links the Khumbu Valley with the Gokyo Valley, traversing a high pass with a glacier. Under good conditions it can be completed by any strong trekker; after heavy snowfall it may be unsafe, but there is a fallback 'long way round'. We describe the link in the westerly direction, for those descending from Lobuche, but it works equally well going eastward from Gokyo.

Chola Tsho, with Taboche and Cholatse

Lobuche (4910 m) to Dzonghla (4600 m)

- From Lobuche, divert from the standard descent path by bearing right 1 km south of Lobuche. Enjoy the gentle traverse as it heads slightly uphill, with great views back up the moraine, and also across the valley to Dughla and Pheriche with Ama Dablam and other peaks.

- As you round the shoulder of Arakam Tse westward, you gain amazing views over the glacial Chola Tsho lake, with the craggy peaks of Taboche and Cholatse as backdrop.

- The path swings right, westward, but remains easy walking across an area with many streams. After crossing the largest of these, you begin your final uphill approach to Dzonghla, almost hidden in its valley.

- There's a couple of lodges here, but facilities are fairly primitive: don't count on an inside toilet. However, you may well see snowcocks strutting their stuff and it's pleasantly quiet here.

Dzonghla (4600 m) to Thangnak (4700 m) via the Cho La (5368 m)

- Plan to set off very early for the Cho La: rockfalls and avalanches are a real danger later in the day once things have warmed up. Also, if there has been recent snowfall, the terrain may be very hard going or even treacherous, and crevasses in the glacier could be hidden by snow: take great care. In adverse conditions, the route may even be impassable. Take local advice before deciding to set out.

- The early morning mountain views are sensational, with Cholatse to your left and the Lobuche ridge to your right. The photo at right shows Cholatse towering over morning mist soon after dawn.

- Begin by climbing uphill, gently at first, but the valley soon narrows. The trail turns into a series of stiff zigzags leading to a steep-sloping rock and boulder field, with large slabs pointing toward a seemingly impregnable wall of jagged mountains.

Cholatse (6440 m)

- Gradually it emerges that the route will win through diagonally uphill. Keep close to the rock wall at your left, and stay close as the route veers to the left. Although the terrain isn't easy, this section merely needs persistence and stamina.

- Finally you top out at the surprisingly level glacier. This can be fairly easy going, as long as the snow isn't too deep and soft. Keep to the southern edge of the glacier and stay alert for crevasses and frozen ponds.

Porter crossing the glacier

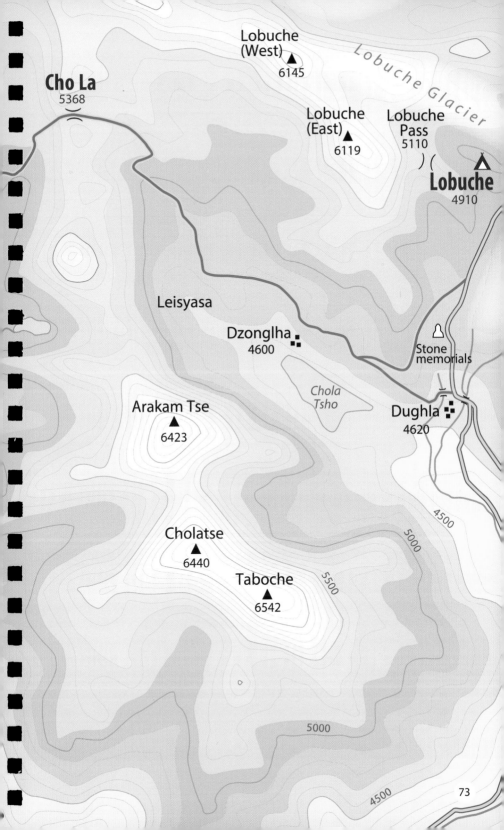

Lobuche
(West) ▲
6145

Lobuche Glacier

Cho La
5368

Lobuche
(East) ▲
6119

Lobuche
Pass
5110

Lobuche
4910

Leisyasa

Dzonglha ▪▪
4600

*Chola
Tsho*

Stone
memorials

Arakam Tse ▲
6423

Dughla ▪▪
4620

Cholatse ▲
6440

4500

Taboche ▲
6542

5000

5500

5000

4500

Top of the Cho La

- At the far end of the snow and ice, you finally reach the top of the pass (5368 m/17,610 ft) celebrated by prayer flags, with good views into the valley beyond.

- Reaching this point by no means marks the end of the difficulties. Now you must descend over a steep, jumbled boulder field that seems to go on for hours. It isn't unbroken descent all the way: just after you have crossed a stream and descended to about 4950 m, you have to climb a ridge at over 5150 m.

- Finally, after the strenuous boulder-hopping, you begin a protracted descent on something more like a path, to the right of a major stream all the way down to Thangnak (4700 m/15,420 ft). This settlement, also known as Dragnag, has a couple of lodges with rather more creature comforts than Dzonghla.

Thangnak (4700 m) to Gokyo (4790 m)

- To reach Gokyo, you must first cross Nepal's longest glacier, the Ngozumpa – perhaps the largest in the Himalaya. It's a mountainous, bouldery and scree-covered glacier, not remotely like the gentle flat glacier atop the Cho La, and like all glaciers, there are possible dangers.

- The normal way of doing so is to descend westward from Thangnak and to cross to a cairn on the crest of the moraine. From here, cross the glacier as directly as possible and climb to the moraine on the far side. The glacier traverse is undulating and rough, but when this route is viable, the whole crossing may take only an hour or so.

- You emerge at a point just north of the First Lake – a distance of just over 1 km. You turn right to hike past the Second Lake and into Gokyo: see page 67.

- When the local advice is to avoid this route, the alternative is likely to take rather longer. This alternative heads north-west for nearly 2 km along the lateral moraine from just below Thangnak, a surprisingly slow hike.

Overlooking the Dudh Pokhari lake

Once you head west across the glacier, progress is still slow but you emerge on the glacier's western lateral moraine, soon reaching a wonderful vantage point over Gokyo's Third Lake (Dudh Pokhari).

From here it's a short descent into the village with its welcome facilities. And if you are still hungry for more summits, you can always climb Gokyo Ri from Gokyo: see page 76. For the descent from Gokyo to Namche, simply reverse sections 4·1 to 4·3, with faster times because you are acclimatised, and (on trend) descending.

Gokyo, from the slopes of Gokyo Ri

4·5 Ascent of Gokyo Ri

South-east to Cholatse and Taboche

For many trekkers, climbing Gokyo Ri (5357 m/17,580 ft) is the prime goal of visiting Gokyo. The altitude gain above the village is 567 m/1860 ft and the round trip takes about 3-4 hours plus summit time. Compared with Kala Pattar (see page 59), both start point and 'summit' are slightly lower, and the final approach not nearly as strenuous, so it's a slightly easier climb although it takes a similar time. In both cases, the reward in clear weather is a stunning view of the world's highest mountains, in this case enhanced by views over the turquoise lake and Nepal's largest glacier.

Summit panorama: Everest, Lhotse and Makalu (distant), with Cholatse and Taboche towering above the Ngozumpa Glacier

Sunset over Everest and Lhotse

Start on an obvious path from the north of the village that climbs sharply north-west. The steep gradient is unrelenting in its central section, but pace yourself according to fitness and acclimatisation. What you finally reach isn't a true summit, but rather a level area from which the panorama becomes complete. Nevertheless, at altitude it still calls for quite an effort. Many people climb Gokyo Ri in the late afternoon to catch sunset over Everest: don't forget your headtorch for descending in the dark.

The summit view differs greatly from Kala Pattar's. From this greater distance, Everest (8848 m) is clearly taller than Lhotse (8516 m) to its right, whereas Nuptse (which dwarfs Everest from Kala Pattar) seems to merge with Lhotse. In clear conditions, you will see four of the six highest peaks on earth, indeed three of them are visible in the photo below, with Cho Oyu (8201 m) lying almost due north.

To the right of Everest, Lhotse and Makalu (8481 m) are the jagged teeth of Cholatse (6440 m) and Taboche (6542 m), towering over the glacier. Our front cover photo was taken from here.

5 Reference

Mountain People

Profits from the sale of this book are being donated to **Mountain People**, a well-respected charity that helps mountain people to help themselves: ***www.mountain-people.org***. Mountain People was founded by David Durkan and is a registered organisation in both Norway and Nepal, with voluntary boards. Its patrons include Sir Chris Bonington. Mountain People mainly works through joint projects, but after a disaster it gives direct aid to people in urgent need. Its work after the 2015 earthquakes is documented in *Earthquake Diaries*: see below.

Organisations and media

For other useful websites, including porter protection, altitude medicine and tour operators, please visit our links page at ***www.rucsacs.com/links/tte***. We also list there various media websites on a wide range of themes from landing at Lukla, through plate tectonics to using Google Earth to 'fly to' Everest.

Books

Everest has atttracted a vast literature, especially about successes and failures in attempts on the summit. The list below is a small, personal selection.

Earthquake Diaries Siân Pritchard-Jones and Bob Gibbons (2015) Expedition World 978-1-514834-19-0

A contemporary account of May 2015, when the authors were in Nepal to help with disaster relief from the 25 April earthquake (Richter 7.8). They lived through the May 12 quake (Richter 7.3), continuing their relief efforts, and they tell the inside story of the response, including the stoicism and resilience of the Nepali people. Compelling reading, llustrated with 150+ photographs.

Everest: Summit of the World Harry Kikstra (2009) Rucksack Readers 978-1-898481-54-6

A visit to EBC may whet your appetite to understand how climbing Everest is attempted. This book tells the full story realistically – the dangers, details of oxygen calculations, downtime and boredom in tents – as well as the thrills of summitting.

Into Thin Air: *A personal account of the Mount Everest disaster* Jon Krakauer (1997) Pan Macmillan 978-0-330-35397-7

A best-selling insider account of May 1996, when five expeditions set off for the summit in apparently good conditions, but a tragic combination of events leads to eight deaths including two team leaders, Rob Hall and Scott Fischer. The 2015 movie Everest re-tells this story, and although Krakauer has criticised aspects of the film, his own account and role have also caused controversy.

Nepal Trekking and Great Himalaya Trail Robin Boustead (2nd ed 2014) Trailblazer 978-1-905864-60-7

Guidebook to many trekking routes including the recently established Great Himalaya Trail, of which the Nepal section takes 90-160 days.

View from the Summit Ed Hillary (2000) Corgi Books 978-0-552-14694-4

These are the memoirs of a modest man who always shared credit for his famous first ascent of Everest with Tenzing Norgay, and who followed up with a programme of building schools, clinics and bridges in Nepal. He describes later adventures, included taking a team of tractors to the South Pole and jet-boating up the Ganges, and documents how his ability to acclimatise declined sharply with age. His book includes thoughtful reappraisal of the dangers of pushing the limits of human effort.

Maps

Below are our two favourite maps, but you can buy other maps cheaply in the shops of Kathmandu.

National Geographic's Adventure Travel Map *Everest Base Camp* (2004) 978-1-5669-5519-5

This map is waterproof, rugged and revised periodically; the main mapping covers all treks in this book at 1:50,000 with 50 m contour interval; its reverse carries a street map of Kathmandu (with a Thamel enlargement) plus a small-scale Nepal map.

Everest, Gokyo, Three Passes Himalayan MapHouse/Nepa Maps (updated 2014) NE517 978-9-993347-94-1

Clear mapping with scale 1:50,000, contour interval 40 m and colour coding for the Three Passes Trail (a 3-week circuit from Namche via the Renjo La, Cho La and Kongma La).

Acknowledgements

We thank Siân Pritchard-Jones and Bob Gibbons for their in-depth expertise on Nepal and their willingness to field our many queries from a great distance. We thank Richard Struthers for supporting one of our treks in Nepal and warmly recommend his company Safe Journeys: *www.safejourneys.co.uk*.

Photo credits

The first 10 photos are credited to **Dreamstime.com** jointly with named photographers: front cover and pp65, 76 (upper) and 77 (upper) **Daniel Prudek**; pp4-5 **Vermacht**; p20 (lower left) **Thavorn Chaisuwannakorn**; p31 (lower) **Dimaberkut**; p44 (upper) **Byelikova**; p66 (lower) **Kshishtof**; p74 **Catherine Falconer**; p16 (upper) **www.steripen.com**; pp76-7 (lower) **Paul Krueger**; p23 and p29 (lower) **Siân Pritchard-Jones** and **Bob Gibbons**: all 85 other photographs, including title page and back cover, are by **Jacquetta Megarry**.

Get by in Nepali

ba dail!	congratulations!
bujh-yo	I see
dhan-ya-bad	thankyou
ek-chin	just a minute
gu-**hahr!**	help!
ha-**jur!**	please explain/say again?
hos **gar**-nu-hos	be careful
kah-ne **pah**-ni	drinking water
kah-ti paisa?	how much is it?
kah-to-rah!	great!
koh-la, ko-si	river (as in Dudh Kosi, Imja Khola)
ko-ho?	who is it?
la	pass (as in Cho La)
mahf **gar**-nu-hos	I'm sorry (I apologise)
mai-le bu-**jhi**-na	I don't understand
ma **mahn**-chu	I agree
mero naam ... ho	my name is ...
na-ma-**ste**	hello/goodbye/greetings
ri	peak (as in Gokyo Ri, Pumori)
shau-**cah**-la-ya **ka**-ha-cha?	where's the toilet?
ta **chai**-na	I don't know
tas-bir **kik**-nu-hun-cha?	may I take a photo?
tik cha	OK

Index